a story of finding light in the dark night of the soul

WINCHESTER HAGANS

Printed in The United States of America
ISBN 978-1-7986-5469-9

This book is dedicated to all who have
tasted both a gun and grace

Do not believe the lie that you are alone.
Do not give up.
You will make it home; I can't wait to see you there.

Table of Contents

Forward

I am a reader of books. I have read many; some of them were good, a few changed my life.

My son, Winston Chester, we call him Winchester, has written his first book. It is, I believe the first book anyone in our family has written. I believe it is a good book. I think, in fact I am quite certain that Winchester's book, *LUX*, will be one of these rare works that holds the power to change men's lives.

In the Bible one of God's titles, one of His given names is 'The Word'. God is the one whose words created life 'in the beginning'. It is God's words, a whisper breathed upon Adam's face that brought him to life. Our first cry outside the womb is an echo of that first cry, and a memory of that first 'word' breathed upon man. In the New Testament, John 1:1 & 14 to be exact, it is written that, "In the beginning was the Word, and the Word was with God and the Word was God…And the Word became flesh and dwelt among us…" That must've been something special, but we missed it. And because we missed it then, God has continued to send men and women to remind us of that Word. We call that Word, Jesus. And we call men and women who strive to show us all the brutal beauty and lingering love that first Word held, we call these and women writers, authors, and echoes of the first Word.

Winchester Hagans is such a writer, an author, an echo. His first book, *LUX*, is a shadow of that first created light. His words echo many, many others he has read himself, some perhaps his dad read to him.

As a reader of books and a father to a writer I guess I can best describe Winchester's *LUX* as a modern-day, hippie-hipster, honest reckoning of St. John of the Cross' 'Dark Night of the Soul'. It is brutally, beautifully, and sometimes breathtakingly honest and as such an echo of that first life giving breath.

So take a deep breath, open the pages and follow an honest man down a long, hard road. You never know what might be waiting for you at the end of the road. The joy is always in the journey.

A Servant,
Rick Hagans
Winston Chester's ~~Dad~~ Pops

Introduction

As I am sitting here to write this it is late. Most likely tonight will be yet another one which finds me writing till the witching hour. But if you continue to turn these pages you shall find that this is an often occurrence for me when writing.

I started the project which would turn into this book roughly 8 to 9 months ago. I started because of my dear friend Bryan Joy. He is one of those friends who truly knows me; the good, the bad, the grace I have received, and the reasons why I needed to receive it. As I would often do while on the phone with him, I would joke that one day I would write a book about all that God had brought me through and taught me in what has been the darkest/hardest season of my life thus far. And usually he would joke back that one day I should. But this time he didn't say that, this time he told me to either write it or stop saying that I would 'one day'.

Over the next few months I spent countless hours sitting in front of a beat-up laptop. For every word that you will find here there is at least another that was deleted. But in the end, I was able to put together what you have in your hands.

This book is something of a misfit, a ragamuffin; because this book is something of me. And I hope to be considered nothing more than one of Abba's ragamuffins as one of my heroes was. This book is my story. In these pages I will confess to you much of my sin, my doubt, my fear, and much of my hope that I found despite it.

I know that there will be some reading this that don't appreciate radical honesty, especially in the Church. If that is you, I would like to thank you for reading this far, but I would ask that you simply place this book down and pick up something else. Because if you don't you will become angry with me. Or maybe, just maybe, you will end up finding that you are a ragamuffin like me. Which is the scarier, but better, of the two options. In this book I admit to drinking too much (too often), sleeping with someone as a Christian single, looking at porn, and a few other things. I think my DUI is page three... But each of these, at their root, are truly nothing more than doubting God, being angry with God, running from God, and not trusting that I was who God said I am. In reading this some of you will want to label me a hypocrite, and you'll be right. But lucky for both of us radical grace is offered to even hypocrites like me...and you.

So what you hold in your hands is nothing more than my life. I hope that there is something of my story which gives you hope and leads you back to, or maybe for the first time to, Jesus. The real Jesus of the bible. Not the white, anorexic, whippy Jesus of the Western World's imagination or the Jesus of a political party that just so happens to hate all the people they hate as well. I hate that Jesus.

Often in the Church we are conditioned to hide our pain, our shame, our doubts. But here I do all that I can to place mine in the forefront. And I will call you to follow me in doing so.

In all honesty there is a part of me that still thinks that it's not too late to keep this book to myself. This is because I am still wrestling with the fear that once you read this, you'll think differently of me. Assuming that you have ever thought of me before picking up this book. If you finish this book you will know more of my sins than my own momma knows as I write this.

But through this season, my dark night of the soul, I have had a number of men, brothers given to me as a gift of my adoption, who have known each sin listed in these pages and more. And through that I have found that it is only once we are able to truly take off our mask and give ourselves permission to feel what we going though and confess to what we have done that we are able to start finding healing[1].

In the last book we are told that those in heaven have conquered the enemy by "the blood of the Lamb and by the word of their testimony[2]". Often in the church we have compartmentalized someone's testimony to the story of how Abba adopted them and how the Holy Spirit brought them to Christ. But to do so is a disservice to both my testimony and to yours. Our testimony covers all of what Christ has done, and is doing in our lives. Our testimony is the sin that we saw defeated last week and the sin that we have been given the grace to fight tomorrow.

This book is my testimony of the past 2 and a half years. My sin. My doubt. My fear. My failure. And the radical grace and power of a loving God who decide that those things would not have the last say in my story, even when I wanted them to.

---

[1] Thanks Pastor Brad for calling me to this each time I spoke to you in this season. I hope you know how much you mean to me. How much your words have been nothing less than life.

[2] Revelation 12:11

I also believe that we see in Scripture that one of the things that each believer is called to do is to strengthen the faith of others in the family. Paul even refers to this as a spiritual gift to be imparted to others[3]. And I believe that one way that this is done is by sharing our story. Our stories of how great our sins actually are, and how much greater the grace of Christ always is. For those of us who belong to Christ, we are not our own[4]. And that means that all of who we are belongs to Christ, and as we know, all that Christ has He gives to us, the Church. And that includes our stories. Even the parts of it we wish that we could keep hidden.

I would also like to let you know that in the pages of this book I have chosen to capitalize each time I am referring to the LORD. So often you will see things such as a capitol 'H' for he or him in the middle of a sentence. Or perhaps a capitol 'Y' for you or your, especially in the prayers that accompany each chapter. This is purposeful. I have also chosen to use a capitol 'H' when speaking of Heaven and calling it home. Though I can at times forget it in my writing I have long tried to do this. I began doing this years ago while reading *The Humor Of Christ* by Elton Trueblood, which I highly recommend. So as a defense for my reasoning I will simply quote Trueblood and give his reason as my own. As he is a wiser man and a better writer than I. "I understand why some authors do not capitalize pronouns referring to Him (Jesus), but I feel more loyal when I employ such capitalization.[5]"

---

[3] Romans 1:11
[4] 1 Corinthians 6:19-20a
[5] Trueblood, Elton. "Preface." *The Humor of Christ*, Harper & Row Publishers, 1964, p. 12.

LUX

I hope and pray that this book shows you that no matter how dark it has gotten, light always comes after darkness for the believer. For we know that in Christ 'was life, and the life was the light of men. The light shines in the darkness, and the darkness has not overcome it.[6]"

-a chosen sinner,
Winchester Hagans

[6] John 1:4-5

I
Confession

"Be gracious to me, O Lord, for I am in distress; my eye is wasted from grief; my soul and my body also. For my life is spent with sorrow, and my years with sighing; my strength fails because of my iniquity, and my bones waste away…But I trust in you, O Lord; I say 'You are my God.'"
- Psalm 31:9-10, 14

"We were promised sufferings. They were part of the program. We were even told, 'Blessed are they that mourn,' and I accept it. I've got nothing that I hadn't bargained for. Of course it is different when the thing happens to oneself, not to others, and in reality, not imagination."
–C.S. Lewis

Before we begin, I have a confession to make. I am broken.

Maybe that makes you want to place this book down before you begin. But I believe that if you are honest, there is part of you that is broken as well. I believe this because when we get to the place where we can be truthful with ourselves, we are all broken people in some shape, form, or fashion.

For a long time I worked as hard as I could to be 'ok'. And maybe you are reading this as someone who is trying for the same end. Even more than ok, I wanted to be good. I had a theology that said I was a sinner saved by grace alone. I theologically believed that anything good in me came from Christ, but practically I thought I was doing pretty well. And if you took the time to talk to me I would try and make sure you knew that.

At 24 years old I felt as though I had a pretty good resume under my belt. Right after high school I had moved to NYC and interned with Times Square Church; I was just a janitor, but I talked it up like I was more. Somehow, foolishly believing that a janitor was a less godly a position than a pastor. (Please note that I am not talking down the job of being a maintenance workers and janitor, Earl Stocker was the head of maintenance at that church while I was there and he is one of the best damn men I have ever met. Better than the majority of pastors I've met.) I was able to live in Ireland for a little over a year after that and work at a church in Cork City. Then I worked for my father's non-profit where I planned and led mission trips for a few years. At 22 I was co-pastor of a SBC[1] church plant. I wrote the Statement of Doctrine, the Bylaws, a membership covenant, and membership class (although we never ended up going with covenant membership, much to my sugrin). At 24 I had around 500 hours of preaching under my belt, and a few of those hours were to crowds of a few thousand. However I often left out that the vast majority was to groups of less than 100. Again, foolishly thinking that my time spend in front of large crowds was far more important than the time spent elsewhere.

I had big dreams, and though my theology bellowed out that was nothing but a tool that God could chose to use, or not to use. I started to believe that I must be a pretty good tool, because He seemed to be using me a lot. And it was with a heart full of pride that, at 24, I moved west.

I moved to Albany, Oregon with high hopes of starting and completing a church-planting residency with a church there and then move back to NYC to plant a church with the Acts 29 Network. And not only was that my plan, but I knew that I would grow that church. I had no doubt in my mind that in just a few short years you would know my name. I was damn prideful, although I honestly didn't see it just quite yet.

---

[1] Southern Baptist Convention

Looking back, I'm not really sure how I missed all the red flags that God was clearly showing me about the state of my heart. But then again, looking back I see that I ignored more than just the red flags of my pride. But, if you keep reading I'll get around to a few of the other ones before this book is done.

I also realize that at this point what I have said can sound almost like a humble brag. But I want to get to the place that you can understand the fortunate fall that was waiting for me just beyond the horizon. Being brought low doesn't hurt so much unless you believe that you have climbed quite high.

Getting to Oregon was great. Everything was starting to take shape for the church-planting residency that I was starting. My first month there I sat down with the pastors and we had a timeline that started as I sat in that office and ended with a church in Brooklyn. *My* church. The first few months there I got settled into the church, I got a job, a place to live, I was even talking with my then girlfriend about her moving out west to join me. My life was, more-or-less, everything that I wanted it to be.

Then as my first summer in Oregon rolled around God decided to shake me a little harder. He fired the first warning shot across my bow to let me know that something was coming. One night driving home I a saw flashing lights behind me and got pulled over. I always tried to make sure that I was careful when I went out for a few pints. I had a rule that I would only have two or three drinks if I was driving. And that was three drinks spread over some time mind you. But I had forgotten to factor something into the equation, forgotten or just not cared to think about, in Oregon some beers are pretty strong. I'm talking 12-14+ percent strong. Being from Alabama that wasn't something I was used to. The south is picking up their beer game, but Oregon has been in it for a good long while. And these aren't the type of beers that taste bad because of how strong they are, they are the types of beer that are dangerous just because of how good they taste.

But that night in Oregon, I got pulled over. I went to jail. And to make it all the worse the only people I knew in Oregon I knew because I was the kid who moved there to work at the church they went to. So it was my pastor who picked me up from jail. I had left him a voicemail and prayed that he got it. He did, and to make it worse he saved it. Though it brought such shame to me over and again, he would lovingly play it back to me from time to time. I thought he was doing it to shame me, to somehow put me in my place. Each time I heard my own drunken voice I would cringe. But looking back I believe that he did it for another reason. I think it was because he had understood something that I hadn't quite gotten at 25 years old. Something I'm not sure I completely understand now, but something that I am chasing after.

In his book *The Ragamuffin Gospel,* Brennan Manning puts it like this, "We must know who we are. How difficult it is to be honest, to accept that I am unacceptable, to renounce self-justification, to give up the pretence that my prayers, spiritual insight, tithing, and success in ministry have made me pleasing to God! No antecedent beauty enamors me in His eyes. I am lovely because He (God) loves me. Honesty is such a precious commodity that it is seldom found in the world or the church. Honestly requires the truthfulness to admit the attachment and addictions that control our attention, dominate our consciousness, and function as false gods."[2] I was someone what had formed his identity around Christianity, but Abba God was starting the process that

---

[2] Manning, B. (2000). Tilted Halos. In *The Ragamuffin Gospel*(pp. 83-84). Sisters, OR: Multnomah.

would strip from me every false god that I had trusted in. It started in that jail cell on a summer night in Oregon, and I believe that it will continue until my prayer of Maranatha[3] is answered or Jesus takes me home.

As time passed I learned how to avoid certain topics with certain people. I felt the shame of what I had done. Theologically I knew that the grace of Christ covered even that sin, but I also 'knew' that I had to work to show Him that I would be better. I would do what was needed so that it wouldn't happen again. He would give me grace, but I would show Him that I would pay it back. Looking back now, I feel more shame about that than I do about my DUI.

That was the start of the journey that I am now on. Though I am not necessarily proud of it, that was the start. I did not see it at the time. But in the following year, almost to the day, God would take away everything that I put any stock in. Anything that I based my identity on, or placed my hope in, He would take away from me. And He wasn't even nice enough to ask if I was willing to part with these things that I clung to.

So jumping forward a year, that girl that I had wanted to follow me to Oregon had instead persuaded me to head back to the heart of Dixie. Now, being some time removed from that day, the timing was almost comical. Almost. But by this point she was more than my girlfriend. We had already placed deposits and invited friends and family to celebrate us on a fall day in September. I had just moved back from Oregon. I had either given up, or had taken away from me, the plan to finish my residency in Oregon. The pastor up there, the same one who picked me up that night I got

---

[3] This is the Greek word at the end of St John's Revelation which is translated 'Come Lord, Jesus.' Revelation 22:20

arrested, had talked with other pastors about me moving somewhere else to finish my residency with another church. But at this point what seemed most important was to make sure that the life I was planning didn't allow ministry to come between me and the person who I was planning on making my family, as I have seen happen so often in the church. So each time an offer came up it was eventually turned down, with not so much as following up. She wanted to live in Alabama, so we would live in Alabama. I packed up all I could fit in a small Uhaul trailer, and what I couldn't fit ceased being mine. I drove back to Alabama. Even driving 32 hours straight on the last leg, fueled by coffee and a desire to a pretty girl with curly hair.

It was when I was returning the Uhaul when I got the call. The call that said that we would need to see if we could get back those deposits that were made. And it seemed to drag out. I spent the rest of my summer trying to fix things, and she spent the summer not seeing me. At the end of it all my engagement ended over the phone like a bad jr high relationship. I even had to pick up a diamond ring from the local post office. Looking back I'm still not sure what all happened. Why I could be so sure and be hit with this out of the blue. But in hindsight this relationship was, like my DUI, full of red flags that chose I ignore. We would try to pursue Christ together, but when we had our breaks from long distance I never actually stayed in the guest bed. And through that summer my lack of ability to control and/or fix what was wrong drove me to anger. As Timothy Keller wrote, "Ordinarily when our love is rejected we get angry, retaliate, and do whatever we can to diminish our affection for the rejecting person so we won't hurt so much."[4] And looking back I was doing just that. I felt rejected, betrayed, unloved,

[4] Keller, Timothy. "The Two Lost Sons." *The Prodigal God: Recovering the Heart of the Christian Faith*, Penguin, 2008, p. 23.

shamed, and so many other things. In an attempt to fix myself I tried to simply stop hurting.

That summer I prayed, I fasted. I did everything that *should* be done to make God to fix things. I held up all that I had done for Him and knew that He owed me this one. I had trusted Him, so He would deliver. But I didn't just want Him to deliver me; I wanted to tell Him how to do it.

While I was still on my road trip moving from Oregon back to Alabama I was joined by a friend for the long drive. Looking back he was a funny choice, he's originally from the Bronx in NYC and had never slept in a tent before that trip. And my plan was to camp from the great Northwest all the way down to the heart of the South. But when we arrived in Yellowstone National Park and I began to look for campgrounds, he snuck off to rent a cabin for the night. The next day or so we were in the Badlands. I'm not sure if you have ever been to the Badlands in South Dakota, but it's somewhere I hope to get back to. While driving through land that was carved by God Himself, as if to simply show off that He could, I remember telling my friend that I felt that God had taken everything out of my hands. He had taken everything but this girl…

After I got back to Alabama and the summer went on, I began to attend a local Presbyterian Church. It was close enough to walk to, which was good for me.

Late one Saturday night that summer I tried one more time to pray. But as this season progressed most of my payers quickly turned to anger or tears. But I would try once more.

It's funny how sometimes God orchestrates things just the right way at just the right time. It's almost as if He's sovereign, or something like that… I had earlier in the week met with a local pastor who had started a counseling center as his way of retiring. Looking back over the history of the church, men of God never really retire. They seem only to keep going, destined to die with their boots on. While meeting with him, he told me that when I struggled to pray in this season that I should simply find a song or two that I could sing as a prayer to God. And I think that Jesus is ok with that.

That night on the porch I sat and shifted between hoppy beers and Ethiopian coffee. Sometime around 2am I finally let the dam break. A song came on my playlist from a worship band that I like. And I don't like a lot of them. It seems to me that most Christian bands these days are either asking Jesus to go to prom with them[5], or they have decided that theology no longer matters once you dim the lights and get people to sing along. But sitting there two songs[6] began to pierce me, and caused me to bellow out in honest cries that I had thought for a few weeks, but never had the courage to admit out loud. Even when no one else was around.

I didn't believe Jesus anymore. I had preached the faithfulness of Jesus on four continents. I had hinged the trajectory of my life on the lone fact that Jesus could be trusted. And yet, alone and in the dark of the night, I let the words roll off my tongue. I sat on my porch I played those two songs on repeat. The words were honest and they cut to the deepest parts of me. If you have not listened to them I would ask that you place this book down and do so. I have footnoted the names of the songs and the bands. Seriously, pull the smart phone from your pocket and look up these

---

[5] A Phrase that I first heard Mark Driscoll use while he was still the teaching pastor of Mars Hill Church in Seattle, WA.

[6] The songs were 'A Prayer' by Kings Kaleidoscope and 'Relent' by Citizens and Saints. The first has a swear word, but I think that Jesus is ok with a cuss word here and there. If you disagree that's fine, but please don't try to make sure I know you disagree.

songs, listen to them and allow yourself to feel the anguish that flows out from each word. Give yourself permission to feel pain, and hope, of each cord.

Writing this I don't know who you are. Honestly I don't know if these words will ever make if off my beat up and cracked computer screen. Perhaps you are someone who is wrestling with your faith. Or maybe you're someone that's not even sure how to be honest enough to admit that you haven't even had the strength to wrestle for a while. We've fashioned a culture in the church where doubt is an act of excommunication, and our pride is more acceptable than our pain. We no longer allow ourselves to be honest about where we are and what is truly going on in our heads and in our hearts. Through the past two years I have learned that the biggest lie told in church these days is, 'I'm doing good.' I can admit that, though Christ has beautifully begun to heal my broken and beat down heart, I am still broken. So I invite you to join me. Be honest enough to tell the truth. It will be the scariest thing that can possibly happen. But it will be worth it.

Christ promised the world that He would return for a Bride without spot or blemish, but have we so easily forgotten that it is He who will clean us. It's so easy to try and fix ourselves with however many steps to a better life. That may draw a crowd on Sunday morning, but come Monday, if we're honest, we've already failed.

Martin Luther said in the first of his 95 Theses that the Christian life was one of continual repentance. And yet somehow we have allowed ourselves to believe that sin is something that happens before we meet Jesus and then goes away. We only allow doubt to be handled by those who we view as 'outsiders'. But in doing this we build a prison for ourselves. And before we know it, we have been walled off like the Count of Monte Cristo, hoping to be free but honestly not knowing if such a dream could ever come true.

As I sat and listened to those songs on repeat I cried as much as I had in the year that came before that night. For the first time in a long time I had come to the place where, not only was I broken, but I could admit that I was broken. And I couldn't see a way of being fixed.

Before I knew it, sitting on that porch, the sun came up. If my life was a movie it would be here that I could point to the foreshadowing placed in by the director. The night would be long, it would hurt. It would hurt a lot. It would take honesty and being alone. It would take a lot of tears and a lot of truth. But it would eventually end. There is a truth that was long ago carved into the Reformation Wall in Geneva, Switzerland and not as long ago carved upon my left arm, 'Post Tenabras Lux". After Darkness Light.

That morning, as I had done before and have done many times since, I walked to 1st Presbyterian Church in Opelika, Alabama. That will ever be one of the services that will be burned into my mind and etched into my soul. The call to worship was given, as is the norm, the band played in a style that I'm not the fondest of. But as they led the congregation in worship I had decided that I would give it all that I had. I would worship. Hands reaching towards heaven, as if I was trying to grab hold of the God who seemed to suddenly be so far away. My cheeks once again wet from tears that somehow had not been let out the night before. And then it happened…

The band began to lead the congregation in that old hymn 'Tis So Sweet To Trust In Jesus'. If you are unfamiliar with the hymn the first two verses go like this:

"'Tis so sweet to trust in Jesus,
Just to take Him at His Word
Just to rest upon His promise,
Just to know, "Thus saith the Lord!"

Jesus, Jesus, how I trust Him!
How I've proved Him o'er and o'er
Jesus, Jesus, precious Jesus!
Oh, for grace to trust Him more!"

As the congregation began to sing I sat down. As much as I wanted to sing along I couldn't. I once heard an old pastor joke that Christians don't tell lies; they sing 'em. In that moment as much as I wished that I could sing along, I knew that such words would be tainted upon my tongue. I had to be honest, and if I was honest, I had to sit down and shut up. I sat on that back pew of my new found home and cried. In the moment I wish that I could have been stronger, I wished that I could have mustered up some more faith. As if that's how faith comes. But looking back, that morning was a turning point for me. I had lived so much of my Christian life trying to be somebody, trying to look a certain way. Especially at 'church'. But that morning I sat down as the congregation sang. Being honest enough about my brokenness not to sing, and bold enough to cry allowed me to be more truthful than singing words I did not mean ever could have.

Though I am not saying that each day since them I have had the same courage to be honest, far from it. But slowly and surely I'm getting there. Not that any of it is my own doing. St Paul tells the church to be reminded that He who started a good work in them would bring it to completion[7]. The days, weeks, and months that followed that day I broke down on the back pew have a mix of good, bad, and grace. Some were truly good days, and some hurt so bad I wanted to die.

[7] Philippians 1:6

Through a lot of different ways Christ reminded me that He was still there, and some days I believed it like I believed the sun was in the sky. And some days I believed it like I believed that bigfoot would be coming over for dinner.

I hope that in reading this you have never been to the place I have been. But I know that some of you have. I also know that some of you may very well be there right now. Some of you may be in the place that you are just now able to be honest enough to admit that you're there. Some of you are still wearing a mask and telling people that you are doing better than you are. And for some of you this place seems like something that other people go through. Some of you may be like I was for so many years, believing that some people went through a 'dark night of the soul' but the closest you would come to that would be by being the person there to help give them light.

Within the pages that follow I can promise nothing but the story of where I was and what God has done, and is doing still, to bring me out. At least I hope I'm out… I hope that somehow you are encouraged. I hope that, if nothing else, you find the courage to be honest with God, yourself, and with others. It won't be easy. Not by a long shot.

If you chose to continue to turn the pages you'll see that by any merit of my own I have no right to even read the word saint. But it's in those places, in the darkness of your own soul that the light of the gospel shines the brightest. If we allow ourselves to stop believe that God is using us because He would be a step behind if He chose someone else, we will never truly value grace. None of us would ever admit to thinking that way. But I did, and I'm willing to bet I was not the only one.

So I invite you to come with me. Come to the place where shame is no longer pushed down and kept in the dark. It's when we are truthful about where we really are, and honest about what we wrestling with that we can truly allow God to take it from us. For how can we let go of things that we can't even admit we have?

So no matter where life has you in this season, I ask you to run to Jesus. Run to Him and be truly honest with Him, maybe for the first time. When we get to the place that we really understand the gospel, running to Christ becomes second nature. Looking back I see the grace of God all over that night on my porch crying out that I didn't trust Jesus anymore. I see the gospel all over that pew that soaked my tears as a congregation sang how sweet it was to trust Jesus while I was asking Him to fix me. Don't get me wrong, those hours were painful, dreadfully so. But looking back I laugh that even in those moments, when I said words that would have made anyone else turn away, Christ came close. I know because through the Spirit I cried out to Him in my darkest night. Matt Chandler once wrote, "The marker of those who understand the gospel of Jesus Christ is that, when they stumble and fall, when they screw up, they run to God and not from him, because they clearly understand that their acceptance before God is not predicated upon their behavior but on the righteous life of Jesus Christ and his sacrificial death.[8]"

So, let's admit that we have all stumbled and we fall far more often than we would care to admit. Let's be honest about how we have screwed up. And let's run to Jesus. It'll be hard, it'll hurt, and it might not be a quick fix. In fact I can promise that it won't be. But we can trust that each time we fall, He'll be there to pick us up.

---

[8] Chandler, Matt. "Moralism and the Cross." *The Explicit Gospel*, Crossway, 2012, p. 211.

As you finish this chapter, and each chapter that follows, I want to invite you to pray a prayer with me. It's not originally mine, but I have made it mine. And I would invite you to do the same. My desire is that you would read the prayer once and honestly wrestle with it. Don't pray this until you can pray it honestly. And when you get to that point I ask that you would. Pray it in a quiet place, and pray it slowly. Allow the Spirit to speak to you while you pray…

PRAYER:

Abba,
You are better than I could ever dare to imagine.
But I am wicked, sinful, miserable, and unable to see rightly.
I know in my head that I should come and confess to You,
But in my heart I still feel the pull away from You and a desire To hide.
I bring myself completely to You.
I give You all of me to do whatever You want.
Break me, wound me, bend me, mold me.
Show me the true face of my sin so that I may hate and run from It.
I have used the body, mind, and spirit You gave me to rebel against You.
In doing so I have misused what you have given to me for my Good and Your glory.
In doing so I have allied with the most evil of enemies against You.
Give me the grace to truly regret my numbed feelings.
Let me quickly learn that the path of sin is a path of hardship, Pain, and trouble.
Teach me that to run from You is to run from that which is Good.
I have seen the beauty and goodness of Your perfect word,
The joy of those who believe it and allow it to lead them,
The righteousness of those who are shaped by it,
And yet I daily act as if Your word is false and I am my own Law.
But even still the Spirit lovingly wrestles with me,
He brings the warnings of Your Word to my mind and heart,
He speak to me through Your everyday providence,
He calls to me through His gentle voice.

And yet I still choose to follow the desires and lust of my own Heart.
And in doing so challenge You to abandon me.
For all these sins I call out and beg that You would forgive me.
Fill me up with a godly grief that trembles and fears You,
Yet one that also trusts and loves You.
Knowing that Your word speaks that those who fear and love You are Yours.
Abba, give me the grace to truly weep over my sins and hate Them.
Let me see clearly the brightness and glories of the cross, even In my darkest night.[9]

[9] Adapted from 'Yet I Sin' in the Valley of Vision Prayer Book

II
Coffee Cup Verses*

"My tears have been my food day and night, while they say to me all the day long, 'Where is your God?'…I say to God, my rock: 'Why have you forgotten me? Why do I go mourning because of the oppression of the enemy?' As with a deadly wound in my bones, my adversaries taunt me, while they say to me all the day long, 'Where is your God?' Why are you cast down, O my soul, and why are you in turmoil within me? Hope in God; for I shall again praise him, my salvation and my God."
–Psalm 42:3,9-11

"And though many storms and floods arise and beat against the saints, yet these things shall never be able to sweep them off the foundation and rock which they are fastened upon by faith. Even though, through unbelief and temptations of Satan, the sight and feeling of the light and love of God may for a time be clouded and obscured from them, yet God is still the same, and they are sure to be kept by His power until their salvation is complete, when they shall enjoy the purchased possession which is theirs, for they are engraved upon the palm of His hands, and their names have been written in His Book of Life from all eternity."
-1689 2nd London Baptist Confession of Faith, Article 17, Paragraph 2

A few years back I was leading a team to New Orleans for street evangelism the week of Mardi Gras. While there I ended up butting heads with a few people at the church we were camped out at, but most of that doesn't need to go here. One of the more memorable times that someone got a more than a little upset with me that was due to my refusal to take 'team shirts' for the group that I brought down. I honestly don't remember much about the shirt, save the scripture that they had used in a design that I'm sure was done by a middle-aged youth pastor still trying to be younger than he was. The scripture that they had chosen for this particular

* I first heard the term 'Coffee Cup Verses' used by Matt Chandler in a sermon. But since I have been listening to him for years I cannot remember which one. You're welcome to listen to them all to find it.

shirt was taken from the first chapter of Habakkuk. "Look among the nations, and see; wonder and be astounded. For I am doing a work in your days that you would not believe if told.[1]" As I tried to politely turn it down and move along with my day I can remember a question being posed to me in shock, "Don't you want to see God do something like this..?" As if God would somehow be prevented from action because I don't have a desire to wear cheesy Christian apparel[2]. But the second thing was a little more disturbing to me. This person read the verse, loved it, threw it on a t-shirt, and never looked any further. If they were to read the very next verse they would have seen that the wondrous things that would happen would be the wrath of God on a nation that had refused to turn from their sin. The amazing thing that people wouldn't believe was that the Chaldeans[3] were coming to invade the land and carry everyone off into captivity.

Needless to say, once I got into this part of the conversation it was the person who was pushing cheesy t-shirts, like a high school drug dealer selling bad weed, who was the one wanting to walk away. Looking back I probably could have given her a lot more grace, and by probably, I mean I defiantly could have. But I had just had a long day around a group of Christians who seemed way too stoked that everyone but them was headed to Hell in a party bus that just so happened to be stopped at Bourbon Street that week. Either that or they were mad that they hadn't been invited to the party. Or maybe it was a little mixture of the two.

---

[1] Habakkuk 1:5

[2] I do own a few Christian t-shirts, but I got them from Righteous Wretch. They are putting out some dope stuff and I would recommend checking them out.

[3] The Chaldeans are also known as the Babylonians, although the Chaldeans were not native to Babylon and ruled at a later date than the first Babylonian Empire

The past two or so years I have really gone back to Psalm 42 over and again. Reading it. Listening to it[4]. It's one that I'm sure you have heard, or at least heard the start of. "As a deer pants for flowing streams, so pants my soul for you. O God.[5]" It's on coffee cups, kitchen towels, cozy sweaters, and framed prints to hang up around your house. A simple search of this verse will result in a plethora of things you can buy, designed with antlers and flowers. After looking at what you can get with this verse on it the designs seem to either target hunters or keep up with the newest bohemian trend. And I mean no disrespect, I have in the past been a very unsuccessful hunter and have had people describe where I live as a bohemian pirate den, although I'm still not 100% sure how I feel about that last part. And now that I think of it, I'm not sure how I feel about the first part either. But needless to say, people love Psalm 42 verse one. And if we are honest, few of us know the rest of the chapter. And even fewer of us like it.

I enjoy a number of types of poetry. One of them is spoken word. Although this particular art form, like most others, is easy to get wrong. Spoken word poetry is beautiful and moving when done well, and annoying at best when done wrong. One of the poets I enjoy is Ezekiel Azonwu; the first poem of his that I listened to is still one of my favorites. The poem is entitled, 'Almost [saved]', and if you have never listened to it I would high recommend doing so. Within the poem the Azonwu says something, "([almost] Christians) can't stand the conviction in Romans, so they sit down to be comforted in Psalms." I understand what he's saying here. And I think that he is getting at something that has honestly become an epidemic in the western Church, a generation of people who only want a happy, fluffy, comforting

---

[4] I would recommend listening to Psalm 42 by the band The Sing Team.
[5] Psalm 42:1

Christianity. But what I don't get is how we have turned psalms into the go-to book for this.

The Psalms are a collection of gut-wrenching cries. Psalms is the book, possibly more than any other save Lamentations, that asks the question, "God, where are you?" And that is the very reason that I have worn a path back to Psalm 42. As verse one seemed to have a great marketing agent, verse three goes straight to the heart of anyone who has ever had their own dark night of the soul. "My tears have been my food day and night, while they say to me all the day long, 'Where is your God?'"[6] We can white wash verse 1 of its pain and anguish, but it would be an impossible feat to do so with verse three. And when we're honest, it's verses like verse three, and an honest look at verse one, that allow us to truly begin to be honest with ourselves, and in so doing, heal.

We have become a culture of people that are ever searching for a 'silver bullet' or 'magic oil' to solve our problems. For many of us, we want to have the desired end without having to go through anything that would lead there. It's why late night infomercials can promise a machine or pill that will give us 6-pack abs without ever having to leave the couch, which in turn will allow us to watch even more infomercials. It's why people leave when things get hard, and why relationships fall apart when it takes work. We have become a people that have believed the lie that everything should be sunny all the time. And when it's not, we feel as though something is wrong. And more often than not, when things look sunny for those around us, we believe the lie that it's because there is something wrong with us. But sometimes we go through dark seasons. Sometimes there are storm clouds in our lives. For a number of months I had a quote from John Bunyan as the background of my computer, "Dark clouds

[6] Psalm 42:3

bring waters, when the bright bring none."[7] Though seeing that quote didn't always bring my heart to a place of rest, it's true nonetheless. Sometimes we need to be reminded that dark clouds come. And sometimes we need to be able to be honest enough to admit that there are a few still hanging over our heads.

One of the hardest things about living in a society that isn't ok with not being ok is that everyone is trying to fix everyone. Though we would never admit it, we functionally act as though Jesus isn't enough of a savior for those around us. And in doing this we try to act as functional saviors for those people, damaging both them and us in the process. I think that this is one of the reasons that we see so many out-of-context verses being used all over western Christendom. We want to have the magic answer to everyone's questions. Are you going through something hard, "For I know the plans I have for you, declares the LORD, plans for welfare and not for evil, to give you a future and a hope."[8] Throw that verse on a coffee cup, give it to someone who's hurting or struggling and we have our magic bullet. But we forget that the plan God had for the people He was speaking to was another few decades of being slaves. They wanted God to say that they could go back home to Israel tomorrow, and instead He told them to throw away their suitcases. They wouldn't be needing them anymore. We want to hope, forgetting that to need hope is an admission that we are, in that moment, hopeless. And who among us wants to admit that we have become hopeless?

I think that, at least most of the time, when people throw out these verses they do it because they really do want to help.

---

[7] I got this from Scripturetype.com which has a great selection hand lettered backgrounds that include Scripture and quotes

[8] Jeremiah 29:11

But so often such things just sting. Or at least they did for me. When we take Scripture out of context it can quickly turn from being a healing balm to feeling like stinging vinegar upon the wounds in our hearts and on our souls. We can take that which God gave for healing us, and we twist it to harm us. Just like we can do with any medicine. If I went to the doctor because I was sick or in pain and was given a prescription I could take the pills and they would work for my good. But that same pill taken out of that context could lead to my destruction. One only need look to the widespread epidemic of people caught in addiction and struggling through recovery due to prescription pills to know this to be true. And in that context it's easy to spot, but in the church it's much harder to see. We have become a people who chase the same kind high as the addict we have told ourselves that we are somehow better than. For in the end, isn't the desire of both to simply feel better? No matter how long that feeling lasts.

While trying to figure out how to place my broken life back together in the aftermath of what I described in the last chapter, people loved to quote Romans 8:28 to me. "And we know that for those who love God all things work together for good, for those who are called according to his purpose.[9]" People would speak this to me and expect me to smile back having all my problems be put perfectly back in place. Though this isn't a book to entirely unpack the theology of the portion of Scripture, I can say that I don't think that Paul wrote this to be quoted to people in pain as a way to avoid the mess of their lives. This verse has become one that people love; they point to it as a promise that everything will work out, and that it'll all be ok. Maybe you didn't get what you wanted but God's got something better.

---

[9] Romans 8:28

Just remember that when God closes a door He opens a window…but sometimes He closes the door and the windows stay locked tight. In quoting this verse people start to make Paul sound more like a mega-church pastor from Houston than the Apostle he was.

If we really allow ourselves the honesty to be broken people, when we get to the place that we can admit that maybe everything won't work out the way we planned or hoped, we can see the beauty of verses like this. In the verses directly following this one Paul tell us why everything will work out for our good. He makes no mention of life feeling ok, at least life here and now. He doesn't give us cheap clichés or try to be our functional savior. He knows full well that our best life is not to be had here and now. He plunges the reader into the depths of eternity past reminding us that for those of us that belong to Christ, He knew us before He formed the world in which we now find ourselves. He desired and pursued up. He predestined[10] us, not according to who we are or what we have or could do. He did this all according to His mercy and grace. And Paul goes further and connects this with our promised future. He points to the fact that all of us who belong to God will be glorified. This word connects us, as the people of God, to the hope of our future home. The New Heaven and the New Earth where we will dwell with God and He will dwell with us with no sin to disconnect us. It's a city so full of God's glory that we won't have need of sun, or moon, or streetlights, or strings of Christmas lights on the front porch. Within two sentences in English he reaches all the way back to eternity past and connects it with eternity yet-to-come, leaving the entire lifespan of the reader pressed in the middle.

---

[10] Merriam-Webster Dictionary defines this word as 'to destine, decree, determine, appoint, or settle beforehand'

Though at times it's hard to keep that in focus. When we are in the middle of a storm we can get to the place where it hurts so bad that such hopes seem foolish. We know that we should look to these things, but they don't help. And so often, when we are honest, a quick examination of our hearts point to the fact that we have stopped seeing God as He is. After my life seemingly fell apart I spent a few months going to see a Christian Counselor,[11] which turned out to be one of the best, and hardest things I had ever done. And I've climbed a few mountains, walked across a few states with my dad, wrestled for years, and even fought people in a cage a few times. During one session he posed a question to me, "Who are you angry at?" He didn't need to ask if I was angry or not. For so often when we allow anger to grow in our hearts it's evident to those around us long before it is ever evident to us. Though we try to keep it under the surface, it makes everything above it boil. Similar to how a hot eye under a pan will cause the water above it to boil, anger will often show itself, whether we see it or not. After all, people don't call them blind-spots because they are so easy to see. In my answer I told him all the people I was angry at. All the people who I felt had hurt me, lied to me, lied to people I loved. I gave my list and felt honest about my answer, but in response he simply asked, "Who else..?" It took me a moment to register and longer to answer. "God. I'm angry at God."

Instead of looking at me like I was less, he simply smiled at me. Almost as a loving father smiles at a child who finally admits what the father already know. He knew I was angry at God. He even admitted to having been angry with God

[11] To say that going to the Owen Center in Auburn, Alabama and meeting with Dr. Gary Spooner saved my life might be an understatement. If you have considered going to a good Christian Counselor I would recommend it. Just make sure that they are Christ based. Simply saying that they are Christian does not mean that is their focus. A lot of people get a Bible verse on their sign to get more presidents in their pockets.

himself for a season, a season while he was pastoring a local church. He let me know that it was ok that I wasn't ok, that he had a season with the same not ok-ness as me. But then went on to how to work through it.

At the heart of all of my pain was that I looked at God and no longer saw a loving Father who would provide for me. I looked at Him and saw someone who was holding out. He had so quickly given to others the thing(s) I desired. I felt like I was the end of a cosmic joke. Somehow I had done something that made Him take it out on me. In my mind He stopped being a loving Father working for my good, but was instead acting like a drunk dad lashing out simply because I was there to be lashed out upon.

So what do we do? If you have been there, or if you are there, what gets us back to the place where we see God rightly? We can try a thousand self-help books; attend just as many seminars (at churches or otherwise) that promise (insert seemingly doable number) simple steps to spiritual wellness. But I think the answer is two-fold, at least it was for me. The first is simply time. When it comes to a physical wound we expect to have a recovery time for the wound to heal, and possibly go through rehab to get back to where we were before. But when it comes to spiritual and emotional wounds we expect it to happen all of a sudden. We want our 'silver bullet', our 'magic oil' to make it all right in a moment, and this isn't helped by churches who claim more miracles each month than the entire book of Acts. But within the time taken, we have to get back to what is true. And to get back to what is true, we have to go to the source.

When Paul writes that all will work for our good he goes on to the end the chapter by rooting such a claim in the love of God for the children He has adopted. He answered the question that I believe that He knew all of us would ask,

'Does God really love me?' or 'Does God still love me?' His answer, inspired by God the Spirit, is to bellow out that there is nothing that can separate us from the love of God that is found in Christ Jesus. Nothing at all. No distance, to power, to circumstance, to sin we commit, or any sins that have been committed against us. And having insight into all of our hearts, the Holy Spirit leads Paul to finish such a bold claim with the words "nor anything else in all creation, will be able to separate us from the love of God in Christ Jesus our Lord.[12]"

Paul tells us in verse 28 that all will work for the good of those who love God, but reminds us that the way it'll work out is that we will get to go Home one day. And even more than that, we get to have the love of God, not just when we get Home but everyday until then.

In connection to the radical love of God that is descried at the end of Romans 8, one of the Reformers penned these words, "He (Paul) declares, that by no length of time can it (our salvation) be effected, (or) that we should be separated from the Lord's favor: and it was needful to add this; for we have not only to struggle with the sorrow which we feel from present evils, but also with the fear and the anxiety with which impending dangers may harass us. The meaning then is, — that we ought not to fear, lest the continuance of evils, however long, should obliterate the faith of adoption…Christ is the bond; for he is the beloved Son, in whom the Father is well pleased. If, then, we are through him united to God, we may be assured of the immutable and unfailing kindness of God towards us. He now speaks here more distinctly than before, as he declares that the fountain of love is in the

---

[12] Romans 8:39

Father, and affirms that it flows to us from Christ.[13]"

Again we see the connection to the love of God towards us, and the promise of a future with Him as our hope. Though I know that it's hard to focus on that.

If we would allow it to, the psalm quoted earlier will give us the honesty to admit that there will still be nights that we'll cry ourselves to sleep. Lord knows I have far more than I would ever admit to. But in those seasons, we cling to the hope that we have a Father who loves us, and a Big Brother, Jesus, who is with us. But sometimes it's hard. Sometimes, if we are honest, we question if we are just talking to ourselves.

Growing up with a dad who was an ordained Southern Baptist evangelist meant that I spent a lot of time at revival meetings; the type that would start Sunday morning and usually last till a Wednesday night service. And being a traveling preacher he had a few sermons that he would use more than once, and a smaller number that he would use even more.

Looking back I'm still not sure why I got in trouble for not paying attention or falling asleep during those sermons. I had heard them before, some I could have even preached for him. My dad is also a storyteller, which made for magical bedtimes growing up. And he still has a way of weaving stories into his sermons in a way that will keep anyone on the edge of their seat, or anyone but a young boy who's already heard them a few times before.

One of his stories was of a young child who's father had already tucked him into bed. A storm rolled in and the

---

[13] Calvin, John, and John Owen. "Romans 8:38-39." *Commentary on Romans*, CHRISTIAN CLASSICS ETHEREAL LIBRARY, p. 286-287.

thunder crashed loudly scaring the young child and causing him to run to his father. The father in the story lovingly explained that there was nothing to be scared of, and if he was scared again to simply remember that Jesus was with him. But the storm got closer, the thunder louder, and the child once again ran scared to his father. And again was reminded, he would suffer no harm due to the storm. And if he was scared to remember that Jesus was with him. Tucked away safely in bed once more, the child was awoken a third time by a strike of lightning that lit up the sky as bright as noon-day and a crash of thunder that would have made the Pacific sound quiet. The child a third time ran to his father. This time the father asked the young boy, "Why are you scared? Don't you know that Jesus is with you?" In answer to the question the boy told his father, "Daddy, sometimes I need a Jesus I can hold onto."

To such a story we may laugh, or say something about the words of children. But thinking of that story now, how often do we run scared because we need a Jesus we can hold onto? Many times when things get hard, it becomes a true test of faith to simply trust. To have hope when hope seems to only let us down.

In the last chapter I told the story of my breakdown while the congregation sang 'Tis so Sweet to Trust in Jesus'. But what I left out was a conversation that I had the following week. I didn't have much going on that week and had been invited up to the church office by the assistant pastor. And later that week spoke with the lead pastor. In speaking to both of these men I admitted what had happened. Even in saying out loud to another person I felt shame begin to choke me like my older brother when we roll Ju-Jitsu. For it is so easy to believe the gospel is true for other people, and so very hard to believe it is true for us. We can easily believe that God's grace will cover a multitude of another's sins, but for some reasons when it comes to ours we would rather believe penance is required.

I spoke to both of my new pastors, and for the first time in my adult life I was starting my tenure as part of a congregation; not as someone who had come to help but as someone who had come needing help. Each of them spoke the gospel over me. But I knew that I had to do something, I knew it couldn't be that easy for me. I told them that I would try to keep that from happening; I even used the excuse that I didn't want to distract anyone from worship. And this was a Presbyterian church, it took almost a year before me yelling 'Amen' in the sermon didn't cause people to turn and look at me like I was swearing at the preacher. I was surprised by the grace that I was given. I was told that if people wanted me to stop being that honest in worship, if people wanted me to pull myself together when I was broken, well those weren't the type of people my pastors wanted at their church anyway. And after two years going there I found that they had already scared off the most of the people who would have cared had I cried each Sunday.

Though it still took me a while to get to the place where I saw it, I had been given a Jesus I could hold onto. He was given to me in the family that He gives all of us who are now part of His family. As part of the Church I was given someone I could hold onto.

I was trying so hard to keep up the appearance that all was well, and in doing so I was falling apart. I couldn't allow myself to be honest, and in doing so I was isolating myself. I had preached grace to others. But when it came to me, I felt the pull to act a certain way, to put the mask of who I once was or who I wanted to be on each time I stumbled off my porch into the larger world. I needed to be reminded of a beautiful truth.

I have no clue where life has you as you read this. But I can assume that, is you have read this far, you are going through a storm or you have gone through one. If you haven't gone through one yet, get ready. We all go through seasons where life lets us know that our plans don't really matter. It takes a million different shapes and forms, but we are a people who will often be caught in the middle of storms. And in the midst of those storms we have to be able to remember who Jesus is, and what that means for us. He is, after all, known for calming a storm or two[14].

As Tullian Tchividjian put it in his book *One Way Love*, "The Gospel of Jesus Christ announces that because Jesus was strong for you, you're free to be weak. Because Jesus won for you, you're free to lose. Because Jesus was someone, you're free to be no one. Because Jesus was extraordinary, you're free to be ordinary. Because Jesus succeeded for you, you're free to fail.[15]"

---

[14] Matthew 8:23-27, Mark 4:35-41, Luke 8:22-25
[15] Tchividjian, Tullian. "An Exhausted World." *One Way Love*, David C Cook, 2014, p. 36.

PRAYER:

Abba,
You know that I am truly unfit to serve You.
You know the deadness that is in me.
You know that I am unable to do anything for Your glory.
You know each place where my heart has grown cold to You
And those around me.
On my own I am weak, ignorant, unsuccessful in things that
Truly matter.
If I am honest I have come to hate myself because of my sin,
And I don't know what to do about it because I feel
abandoned.
I feel as though I never feel Your presence or hear Your
voice Anymore.
I can think back and remember all of my sin and feel the pain
of Each one,
I feel as though all I can do anymore is sin against You. And
I Feel each sin.
Everything I do seems to be wrong, even when I want to do
Right.
Come again and cover me with the floods of your grace.
Even though I don't deserve to be near You, I know that You
Will draw close to me.
Let the very breath I take be a prayer to be more like Jesus.
Let me once again be totally devoted to You.
Let me grow in Your wonderful grace each day more than
the Last.
But Abba, I feel lost when I try to purse these things.
I feel as though I am sinking down each time I try to get up.
Give me the strength to not give up, even if it's only for one
More day.

Give me the strength to hold out hope that You will soon come And deliver me.
For I can't even hope unless You give me the faith I need to do So.
Let me be still, watchful, and tenderhearted.
Abba, I trust You and lean upon You as my only strength.
I need You to lead me and help me in each and every moment.
Let even these trials and temptations become ways to learn to be More like Jesus.
Let even these hard times shape me to serve You in greater Ways,
By teaching me to humbly run to Jesus in all seasons.
Even when it hurts to do so. [16]

[16] Adapted from 'Need of Grace' in The Valley of Vision Prayer Book

III
Bastard Son

"But now that faith has come, we are no longer under a guardian, for in Christ Jesus you are all sons of God, through faith…And because you are sons, God has sent the Spirit of his Son into our hearts, crying, 'Abba, Father!' So you are no longer a slave, but a son, and if a son, then an hear through God."
–Galatians 3:25-26, 4:6-7

"Feeling ripped off and envious, we question the goodness, love, and wisdom of God. Why would he single us out for this treatment? Why would that person (who clearly doesn't deserve it) experience life in abundance? But notice the danger here – we define 'the good life' in physical, horizontal terms rather than vertical, spiritual relationship with God…When you seek identity from a horizontal or tangible experience, you're placing your hope in something that will wither and fade (Isaiah 40:8). Only God outlasts time. Only God avoids decay. Only God eludes chaos. Trusting anything or anyone else is a delusional danger that inevitably will come crashing down." –Paul Tripp

Over the course of going to counseling I would periodically be given homework to do. Sometimes it was fairly easy, and sometime it was much harder. One of the hardest things that I was assigned to do between sessions was to read a section of Scripture and write my own version of it. The text I was given was Lamentations 3:1-27.

"I am the man who has seen affliction
under the rod of His wrath;
He has driven and brought me
into darkness without any light;
surely against me He turns His hand
again and again the whole day long.
He has made my flesh and my skin waste away;
He has broken my bones;
He has enveloped me
with bitterness and tribulation;
He has made me dwell in darkness
like the dead of long ago.

He has walled me about so that I cannot escape;
He has made my chains heavy;
Though I call and cry for help,
He shuts out my prayer;
He has blocked my ways with blocks of stone;
He has made my paths crooked.
He is a bear lying in wait for me,
a lion in hiding;
He turned aside my steps and tore me to pieces;
He has made me desolate;
He bent His bow and set me
as the target for His arrow.
He drove into my kidneys
the arrow of His quiver;
I have become the laughingstock of all peoples,
the object of their taunts all day long.
He has filled me with bitterness;
He has sated me with wormwood.
He has made my teeth grind on gravel,
and made me cower in ashes;
my soul is bereft of peace;
I have forgotten what happiness is;
so I say, 'My endurance has perished;
so has my hope from the LORD.'
Remember my affliction and my wanderings,
the wormwood and the gall!
My soul continually remembers it
and is bowed down within me.
But this I call to mind,
and therefore I have hope:
The steadfast love of the LORD never ceases;
His mercies never come to an end;
they are new every morning;
great is Your faithfulness.
'The LORD is my portion,' says my soul,
'therefore I will hope in Him.'
The LORD is good to those who wait for Him,
to the soul who seeks Him.
It is good that one should wait quietly

for the salvation of the LORD.
It is good for a man that he bear
the yoke in his youth.[1]"

As I read those words I considered various different things; different ways to rewrite it. But as I sat under the weight of these verses it took me a while to be able to re-write it for myself, about three weeks if I remember correctly. But I knew that if I were to write down and read to my counselor what my honest response to these words was; then I would be found out. I couldn't hide behind what little pieces of a mask I had left. I would truly be found out, my brokenness would come full circle and be out in the open once again.

I was eventually able to write, looking at the page now I can still feel the pain of writing it. I can still see the tearstains that are ever marked within my prayer journal. I can flip pages and almost hear the anguish of each word placed by pen upon paper. When asked to look at the anguish of Jeremiah and respond in kind, here are the words that came:

'I have been tricked by the LORD,
He has promised and not delivered what was said.
His word was the light to my path,
but He has led me into the midnight wilderness.
He has caused my heart and my soul to cry out.
In the pain of the moment,
He has driven me to fear what is to come next.
I cry out for help,
and it feels as though He turns His ear from me.
He has told me to call Him Beloved Father,
but it feels as though I have become His bastard son.
You told me that in giving up everything to follow You,
You would give me the desires of my heart.
I followed You, gave You all, and You gave my heart's desires,

---

[1] Lamentations 3:1-27

only to steal them the very moment that they seemed dearest to me.
I have sleep stolen from me,
and rest is kept away.
I sit down to eat,
and hunger is never close by.
I have watered my prayers with tears,
and still I find no answer.
I feel as though I have been forgotten.
I feel as if strength will never again fill me.
But again I will look towards the Throne of Grace.
Once more, and twice after I will be reminded of the gospel.
Though I do not feel you close,
I will remember what is true.
You will never leave nor forsake me.
You will lead me in paths of righteousness for Your name's sake.
You will once again meet me,
and within my weakness You will flex and show Yourself to be strong.
Lord, You have made me weak,
so be my strength.
Lord, I am filled with fear,
so be my courage.
Lord, I feel rejected and alone,
remind me that I am Yours.
Father, teach me to again rest in Your will.
Show me once more of Your love for me.
Let me have patience to allow You to heal me.
Lord, please, let this be to Your glory."

These word were hard to write, and even harder to read. For in reading them I was admitting that I wasn't ok. And on top of that I didn't really see a way that I would be alright any time soon, or possibly ever again. I remember leaving the counseling office that session and being told that maybe after all was said and done, I would have to learn walk with a limp.

At the time I laughed it off. Not me. I was being truthful with my pain; I was being open (at least most of the way, most of the time). I wanted to hear that I was really making progress, that I was on my way to everything being the way I though it should be. That this was but a bump in the road. But instead, he warned that maybe, just maybe, I would walk with a bit of a limp for much longer that I believed. That perhaps my limp would always be evidence that I had been wounded deeply. As Jacob was forced to walk with a limp the rest of his life after his angelic wrestling match. I was bearing my soul and trying to go through everything that I needed to, and the idea that maybe things would not magically get better was slightly depressing. So as I am good at doing, I shrugged it off and told myself that such a thing might be true of others but would not be true of me.

I had allowed something to shift within me. And it took sitting down to write my own lamentation for it to truly rise to the surface. More than anything else I had allowed my view of God to shift. I can't point to an exact moment that this happened. Much like the proverbial frog in the boiling pot, I had remained in the hot water until it was at the point of boiling. And once the water was that hot it almost seemed too much to escape.

It was A.W. Tozer who once wrote that "What comes into our minds when we think about God is the most important things about us[2]." And in that moment what came to mind was someone who didn't care. I had tremendous evidence to the contrary but what I felt in that moment was overwhelming, crippling.

---

[2] TOZER, A W. "Why We Must Think Rightly About God." *KNOWLEDGE OF THE HOLY*, INDOEUROPEANPUBLISHING CO, 2018, p. 1.

Though I would never say it this way, what I was honestly feeling was a since of entitlement. I had done so much for God. I had given up so much to say 'Yes' each time He called me somewhere. I had been a missionary and a pastor. I have moved across an ocean and across a country twice. Well, I guess the second time across the country was more for a girl than for God. But still… I believed that He owed me this one.

Through my relationship with that girl I can look back and see a lot of red flags that I chose to ignore. Growing up I had heard a lot of stories about people who had prayed that they not date anyone until it was their spouse. And when I was 19, living in Ireland, I prayed that same prayer. And over the next 5 years I got close to dating a few people. But I never did. I had never used the word 'girlfriend' until this girl.

We started dating in the fall of 2014 and over the next few months we ended up crossing a few lines physically that I thought that I wouldn't. But I was moving across the country and we were going to make long distance work. In my mind this was God putting space between the two of us. There is no way to stay over at someone's place for the night if their bed was 2,687 miles away. This was God saving us from ourselves. So we stayed together and made a commitment that we would go through a Bible study together, and if we couldn't do that then we shouldn't stay together. So before I moved we both ordered the book, videos, and the workbook for John Piper's *Don't Waste Your Life*.

Each time we set a date to start going through the book some reason came up to push it off, but again it was understandable. I mean I had just moved cross-country and she was starting another semester at university. But we did eventually start, only to have her tell me it took up too much of her time somewhere around chapter three.

Even in this I made peace with it. For I had prayed that I would be single until the girl that was my wife came into my life. And each person I had ever heard speak of praying that prayer also had a story of God answering that prayer. Sure, there were hard times and seasons of frustration. But that was simply the nature of relationships.

There are more examples of red flags that could be given. But to share many more would be speaking someone else's story. And I feel neither the need nor the desire to do such a thing. Each red-flag that popped up I ignored by looking back to that prayer that I prayed for the first time in Ireland, and many times after. Each time God tried to speak to me, I simply responded with telling Him what He should do. After all it was Him who placed her in my life, twice.

Even in the summer months that we were trying to work it out, or the months that I was putting off the inevitable end. I was sure that God would fix it all. This was just a test. I was already playing in my mind the redemptive arch of our story that would inspire our friends and family. I knew that I desired to be a church planter, and in my head I had already planned how we would tell of God 'fixing' all of this to the awe of all who sat in attendance. I was so sure of this I even went ahead and bought my wedding band, and wore it to sleep at night. Falling asleep praying for the end I 'knew' God would give me, for it was the end I 'deserved' the end I was 'owed'.

I can't remember where I first heard it, but I can remember hearing someone once say that we are often mad at God for not giving us things that He never promised to.[3] And that's where I was. I wanted God to promise me marriage to a girl

---

[3] If you know where this quote originated please let me know. I hate forgetting where I heard/read things, but it happens more than I care to admit.

that I loved as much as she let me love her. I am more of a romantic than I let on. I wanted God to promise me a fun, hip wedding that all my family and friends would enjoy and talk of the revelries had for years to come. I had made a plan and had passed if off to God for a signature. I had acted as the congress of my own soul and awaited only the executive signature for my plans to be passed into law.

But as my plans sat upon God's heavenly desk He turned down His signature and instead gave me something which would, in the end, be better for me. But in that moment it felt as though I was simply being wounded once again by the One I trusted the most. And to be candid, it still feels that way from time to time.

As Jeremiah cried out in Lamentations 3, I was wounded. And from my point of view it looked as though it was God who fired the shot.

One of the hardest parts of this process was when I got to the place where I looked back and could only come up with two possible options of what had happened. Either God had tricked me, or I didn't hear from Him at all. And each one of those is more devastating than the other.

All the way back in the garden, the first line ever given to humanity by our enemy was a half-truth veiled in question. Did God really say?[4] It was told to our first mother, Eve. If you don't remember the scene I'll give a brief recap. God had made the heavens and the earth. It was good. He made man, but it wasn't good for him to be alone. So God told him to name all the animals, and none of them was a suitable partner for him. Although I do think it took a good long while to come to that conclusion when he got around to the first dog.

---

[4] Genesis 3:1

So God put our first father to sleep and took a rib from his side and fashioned it into Eve. (I'm still not sure how He did this and had her turn out taller than a Hobbit, but He's God and can do whatever He wants.) When God finally woke Adam and showed him the woman he made to be his bride he broke out in the first ever love song. Which might just be the reason that guys have been trying to learn how to play a guitar ever since.

God officiated the first wedding, and then God said that everything was very good. And to our first parents He gave the whole world and all that was in it, save one thing. There was a tree in the garden, the Tree of Knowledge of Good and Evil. And God told them not to eat the fruit of it. If they did, they would die.

Eventually our enemy came into the garden and asked 'Did God really say?' Our parents ate the fruit; sin entered the world and fractured the cosmos. And with sin came shame, pain, heartbreak, anger, lust, and every other evil and vile thing that haunts our past and wounds our present till this day.

And this is the same thing that our enemy asks us now. Did God really say? Did He really tell you this or that?

Our first parents looked at the law of God and instead of seeing it as protective and covering, they saw it as restrictive. In essence, they saw God as someone who was holding out on them. They began to believe the lie that God was not for them. It's easy to look back and think we could have done it different. But each time we trust our feelings over what God has said we simply place the garden on repeat.

As I wrote my own lamentation I admitted to believing that oldest lie. God wasn't for me. He wasn't Good. He was keeping from me that which would satisfy. The enemy came to me and whispered that age-old lie, and I happily believed him.

I can remember one time when I was younger, traveling with my dad as he went to preach. Though he is ordained through the Southern Baptist Convention he would preach wherever he could, and still does. This particular time he was preaching at a more charismatic church and the sound system had started to mess up. Their reasoning was that it must be a demon in the sound system[5] and if cast out, the problems would be fixed. But the problem was not a demon, or at least not in the sound system. The problem was that they were cheap, and got a cheap sound system.

In telling this story I want to point out two things. I believe that we have a real spiritual enemy and I believe that spiritual warfare is real. But I think that a lot of people give the devil far too much credit. For me, he only needed to lie to me once; after that I began to do his job for him. For I began to tell myself that God was no longer for me, if He had ever been.

I think that if we are truthful, we can admit that we lie to ourselves far more than anyone else does. We say lies over and again to our own souls. I know that people say that we shouldn't talk to ourselves, but those very people tell themselves that saying such things is the right thing to do. A simple reflection of the past 24 hours will bring to light how much we say to ourselves.

And if we are truthful, how often are these words damaging and damning? When we are alone, left with only a dark room at the end of the day, what thoughts come to mind? And

---

[5] I know that most in this camp would not jump to this conclusion, and I am not insinuation that they would, simply telling a story of a single church.

when we sit alone and think of God, or try not to, what thoughts fill our head? Does He love in the narrative that you have written? Is He angry with you? Is He holding out on you? Has He forgotten you?

It's so easy to allow our emotions to control us in moments of extremes. But what truly matters is what is true. If we could step out of the anger or pain of the moment and get a better view, could we spot what's true and what's a lie? I believe that this is one of the reasons that so many of us are good at giving advice but bad at taking our own. For when we are removed from the pain, or lust, or anger, or loneliness of a situation it becomes clear.

It's like driving through a thick fog, not being able to see much farther into the distance than the few feet in front of us.

In looking back over Lamentations 3, Jeremiah allows his heart to bellow out what he feels. He gives himself the room to be honest about what he is going through. For the first 20 verses he makes it known how he feels and whom he believes is responsible. Places like this in Scripture should give us a liberating freedom to be honest, especially in prayer. He even claims that God is the one who wounded him[6] and it was God who filled him with bitterness[7]. But in verse 20 he slows down. He changes his direction and reminds himself of what he knows deep down is true, truer than his situation, truer than even his feelings and emotions. Though even claiming something being more true than our feelings may be heresy in the 21st Century. In verse 21 Jeremiah begins to remind himself that to follow his heart is foolish advice. "But this I call to mind, and therefore I have hope: the steadfast love of the LORD never ceases; His

---

[6] Laminations 3:13
[7] Laminations 3:15

mercies never come to and end; they are new every morning; great is your faithfulness.[8]"

For Jeremiah, and for us, we are allowed to showcase our cares before our Father in heaven. Again, we must get to the place where we are ok with not being ok, but we must do whatever it takes to get back up and keep going. And what it takes is grace, ten out of ten times.

I was speaking with someone on this very issue this evening before I came home to write. In the conversation we spoke about someone we both knew, someone that has become paralyzed by shame. And when we get to those places, honest confession can seems almost worse than death. The command to confess our sins[9] sounds like a manipulative move. For when we are people bound by shame, being found out seems like the worst thing that could possibly happen.

But it is when we confess to people who are committed to us and to the gospel, it is only then that we truly become free. I can remember a while back. I had fallen back into the sin of lust, and this time it led back to a personal demon that I though I had put to death a few years back. In a fight with loneliness and lust I decided to play house with a cute girl that lives in town. The next week I was talking to a dear friend of mine and we could each sense a tension in the air. I was bound by the shame of the sin I had committed. I didn't want to confess because I was scared that if I did he would either cast more shame on me, or simply walk out of my life. But as soon as I confessed it was clear that I would not be met with shame, and that wouldn't retreat out of the messiness of my life. He spoke over me the gospel truth that what I did was a big deal. It was such a big deal that it killed

---

[8] Laminations 3:21-23
[9] James 5:16

Jesus. My sin murdered God. But Jesus died willingly for me. And the same power that rose Him from the grave was now mine. To cover the sin I had committed and to help me go to war with it next time around.

I was scared that within confession I would receive shame, but instead I found freedom.

We should, and have to, work to welcome this. I say work because most of me still hates confession and believe the lies that people will leave when they find out who I really am. But that's something we can talk more about later.

For Jeremiah, he allowed himself the space to be honest, but in the end he came back to what he knew to be more true that what his own heart was speaking. In refocusing our hearts on who God really is we find the freedom that He promises. For God is too good to allow us to go on believing lies about Him for too long. One way or another He will refocus our eyes upon Him.

For me, I have found two ways in which to do this. The first is to go back to Scripture. Through the pages of the Bible we are forced to come face-to-face with the truth of who God is, and the way that He looks upon His children.

You don't need to look very far to see this, but I will list a few that I have often gone to as a reminder of what is true and what is a lie.

"…so that the world may know that You (the Father) sent me (Christ) and loved them (those who belong to Jesus) even as You loved me.[10]"

"The LORD your God is in your midst, a mighty one who will save;

---

[10] John 17:23b

He will rejoice over you with gladness; He will quiet you by His love; He will exult over you with loud singing.[11]"

"for in Christ Jesus you are all sons of God, through faith…And because you are sons, God has sent the Spirit of His Son into our hearts, crying, 'Abba! Father![12]'"

"There is therefore now no condemnation for those who are in Christ Jesus. For the law of the Sprit of life has set you free in Christ Jesus from the law of sin and death.[13]"

"But you are a chosen race, a royal priesthood, a holy nation, a people of His own possession, that you may proclaim the excellencies of Him who called you out of darkness and into His marvelous light. Once you were not a people, but now you are God's people; once you had not received mercy, but now you have received mercy.[14]"

As you read those verses make them personal. So often when we read Scripture we allow ourselves to forget that they are for us. That they speak to us as individual people. When you read allow it to be personal.

Even as the Father loves Christ, and as much as the Father loves Christ, that is how much He loves *me* and cares for *me*.

The Lord *my* God is in *my* midst, a mighty One who will save *me*, He will rejoice over *me* with gladness; He will quiet *me* by His love, He will exult over *me* with loud singing.

---

[11] Zephaniah 3:17
[12] Galatians 3:26 & 4:6
[13] Romans 8:1-2
[14] 1 Peter 2:9-10

For in Christ *I* am a son/daughter of God. And because of that the Father has sent His Spirit into *my* heart so that *I* can come and call Him 'Abba. Father.'

There is now no condemnation for *me* since I am in Christ Jesus. The law of the Spirit has set *me* free.

I am part of a chosen race. *I* am part of a royal priesthood. *I* am part of a holy nation. *I* am God's own possession. And because of this *I* can proclaim the excellencies of God who has called *me* from darkness into light. Once *I* was alone, but God has made *me* part of a His family. Once *I* was given no mercy, but now *I* have received mercy.

The second exercise is that of worship through song. So often we allow this to be isolated to a corporate experience, but it shouldn't be. We should work, and it will be work, to incorporate singing to God into our rhythms of life. Singing along to worship songs all alone is weird. It is. Lets just be honest about it. It'll feel awkward. But how often do you sing along to your favorite songs on Spotify, Pandora, or the radio. If you can do it then, you can do it here. Find songs that are full of lyrics containing gospel truths. Just because a band is labeled under the genre of 'worship' doesn't mean that their words will fill your heart with gospel truths.

So as we look at ourselves, and how we look at God, we can come back to that first line that our enemy spoke and turned it back on him. Did God really say?

He said He loves us. He has pursued us from before the foundations of the world. He has carved (tattooed) our names upon His own hands[15]. He sings over us in joy[16]. He

---

[15] Isaiah 49:16
[16] Zephaniah 3:17

welcomes us in to His family[17]. He is preparing for us an eternal Home free of every pain and wound caused by our sins and the sins committed against us[18]. He will never leave or forsake us[19]. He calls us His beloved[20]. He will fight for us[21]. He will finish all that He started in us[22]. He prepares peace for us, even in the presence of our enemies[23]. Though I could continue I believe that you get the point.

But as we have seen earlier, just knowing this in your head won't heal you immediately. Healing takes time. Healing hurts. But healing happens. So as you go about your days recognize those times you speak to yourself. Take every though captive[24], and work to speak truth to yourself. For whether we like it or not, what is spoken over us becomes our reality, and no one speaks to us more than we do. So let us work to speak what is true.

[17] Romans 8:15
[18] Revelation 21
[19] Matthew 28:20b
[20] Romans 9:25
[21] Exodus 14:14
[22] Philippians 1:6
[23] Psalm 23:5
[24] 2 Corinthians 10:5

PRAYER:

Abba,
Please save me completely from the pain of sin.
I know that I am fully righteous because of the righteousness
Of Jesus.
But I try to fight tooth-and-nail to be more like you on my
Own.
I am Your child and I should look like You.
Give me the eyes to see where I sin and fall short.
When sin calls my name let me not even hear its voice.
Save me from the sin that attacks me and the sin that lives in
My Own heart.
Give the grace and strength to walk as Jesus walked,
Let me walk in the newness of life that You promised,
A life filled with love, a life overflowing with faith, a life
Marked by holiness.
I hate that in this broken world I am filled with brokenness.
I am filled with apathy, apathy, anger, and pride.
Abba forgive me for these things, please kill them for I
Cannot.
I want to believe you, but please have mercy when I don't.
Have mercy on my wandering heart.
When you give me the blessings I pray for I so often make
Them Idols to worship.
Instead of worshiping You for what You have given me I
Worship what You give me.
Please wash me of my adultery against You when I do this.
Close my heart off from all that would cause me to worship
Anything or anyone but You.
For I feel as if I am cursed by this sin.
Let Your victory over sin be ever present in my head and my
Heart,
And let my life show that I truly believe this.

Let me always be fully devoted, confident, obedient, and
Childlike in trusting You.
Let me love You with my soul, my body, my mind, and my
Strength.
Let me love those around me as You have loved me.
Save me from my own temper, my evil thoughts, slanderous
Words, meanness,
And anything in me that does not look like Jesus.
Fill me with grace today. And every day after.
Let my life be a fountain of sweet water.[25]

[25] Adapted from 'A Cry for Deliverance' in The Valley of Vision Prayer Book

IV
Broken Wells

"But as for me, my feet had almost stumbled, my steps had nearly slipped. For I was envious of the arrogant when I saw the prosperity of the wicked…But when I though how to understand this, it seemed to me a wearisome task…Nevertheless, I am continually with you; you hold my right hand. You guide me with your counsel, and afterward you will receive me to glory."
–Psalm 73:2-3,16,23-24

"To be commanded to love God at all, let alone in the wilderness, is like being commanded to be well when we are sick, to sing for joy when we are dying of thirst, to run when our legs are broken. But this is the first and great commandment nonetheless. Even in the wilderness - especially in the wilderness - you shall love him."
–Frederick Buechner

I grew up wrestling. I was never a great wrestler, but I was alright. And if you're not familiar with the sport, one of the aspects of wrestling, for many wrestlers, is cutting weight[1]. My senior year in high school I cut weight from 150lbs and wrestled in the 125lbs weight class. I can still remember one night finally seeing the right numbers on the scale. I took off my sweat suit and the plastic suit that was on under it. I jumped into the shower to wash the sweat off and get ready for bed. But when I got out of the shower I checked my weight one last time, just to be sure. And I was a pound heavier than I had been before I got in.

I had become so thirsty that without thinking about it I drank a pound of warm shower water.

Though a glass of warm shower water doesn't ever sound appealing; I had so deprived my body of the water I needed

---

[1] Cutting weight is the rapid loss of weight, primarily water weight. This happens through a partial dehydration so that a particular weight class can be reached and competed in.

that I drank it anyway. Even without thinking about it. I didn't want to drink it, but I drank it because it was there.

Through this season in my life I have come back to a section of scripture over and over again. It's found near the start of the book of Jeremiah.

"for my people have committed two evils;
they have forsaken me,
the fountain of living waters,
and hewed out for themselves,
broken cisterns that can hold no water.[2]"

The fountain of living water was offered, and instead the hope of these people was in broken wells and dirty water.

These were the people of God. To them belonged the Scriptures, the stories of old that we all wish to have seen. And yet, they turned from God. We can look back now thousands of years removed and ask ourselves how they were so foolish, but when I am honest, and if you dare to be as well, we need only look to our own lives and see the same action.

We read the story, and like 'good' Christians we want to see ourselves playing the part of the weeping prophet and not those who he was writing to. How could the people of God continually refuse to listen to those sent by God begging them to change? Often killing those sent to call them back, and only later to hold them in high regard. But if we look to our own close past, we need only look to the third Monday of January to understand that we do the very same thing.

I'm not sure what it was that brought you to your place of brokenness; sitting here with only a dog at my side I have no

---

[2] Jeremiah 2:13

idea of what caused the darkness to enclose you as well. But as I have said previously, for me what brought it to the forefront was a broken relationship.

Through the feelings of brokenness I wanted nothing more than to simply be 'better'. Not even sure what that looked like. I felt broken, and wanted nothing more than to be mended. And I had no shortage of sermons and books that told me of how to get there. I listened to the sermons; I read the books, and at the end of it…I remained broken. I felt a loneliness that hurt. The type that cannot be explained, only understood by those who have felt it, or feel it now. I wanted nothing more than to have it lifted. I was thirsty in a way that can only be spiritual.

No matter how often I drank from the places I had once found relief, this time around I remained thirsty. So I decided that I would do whatever it took to take that feeling away. I had begged Christ to quench my thirst, to make me whole again. And yet here I was. Still thirsty.

Maybe that's where you are as you read this. Maybe you have done everything that you've known to do. You have taken all the advice that's been given. The advice you asked for, and the advice that you didn't. But it's not working. You feel desperate to simply make the feeling go away. You feel like anything would be better than the pain that you feel. Anyone would be better than no one at all.

That was the place where I had gotten to. I was tired of not being able to sleep when I wanted to and not being able to get out of bed when I needed to.

I was at a place where I wasn't even sure what I wanted. I just knew I wanted something else. And so, like the Israelites and many others before me, I decided to dig my own wells. If

God wouldn't give me what I wanted, then I would find something or someone else who would.

I don't know what wells you have dug for yourself, or what wells you are digging right now. Maybe you're at a place right now where these other wells seem to be working just fine. You're no longer at a place where the world seems like it's falling around you. Maybe you don't feel like you wish everything, or anything at all, was different. But trust me, broken wells don't last that long. And in the end, the best you're left with is dirty water. Which can only satisfy when you are thirsty enough to not care if it's clean or not.

The first well that I dug for myself was an easy one. It was even walking distance from where I moved when I got back to Alabama. I spent a few weeks my first summer back in Alabama where the places I could be found was either drinking with my roommates on my porch, drinking at the local distillery[3], or at 1st Presbyterian Opelika. I decided that if Jesus wouldn't take away this feeling, then I wouldn't feel. It was a place where I felt as though my options were feeling thirsty and broken, staying around people where I could mask my feelings, or not have to feel at all.

But this well soon began to wear thin and dry up. And while still trying to draw relief from a well that was beginning to lose water, or whiskey, I began to dig yet another well. Or maybe I stumbled into a well that has long been one we have all tried to drink from.

One night I was closing down the bar with some friends at the local distillery. And when it closed down we went right next door to the only brewery in town and closed down the bar there as well. We even stayed later than we should have

---

[3] John Emerald Distillery in Downtown Opelika, Alabama

been able to since the owners were with us. And there was a pretty girl who was closing the place down with us as well.

And I'm sure that you can connect the dots from there.

And after a week of staying at her house I realized that this well was also a broken one. What made it take a week was that we both didn't have work that week and played house, more or less. More than just staying there, I enjoyed cooking dinner for someone each night. Watching a movie with someone other than my dog, and playing a board game or two.

I was able to distract myself for a week, to not think about how I felt and what I was going through. But at the end of the week, not only did the well run dry, but it had turned sour. Not that she was a sour person. But now I had not only my brokenness to deal with, but also the conviction of a weeklong affair with a sin I though I would never run back to again.

But isn't that the way it always is.

King Solomon was the wisest man who had ever lived. And through his writing he does his best to drop some knowledge on us. And in Proverbs 26:11 he does what he does all through that book.

"Like a dog that returns to his vomit,
is a fool who repeats his folly."

And I was that fool. Chances are, you have been as well. Maybe not in the same action, but in the same way.

In my head I knew what was right. But I decided that I would look other places. I would find what God wasn't giving me. And I returned to it again. I can still remember when I sat across from the associate pastor at my church and told him of the week that I had. I sat there and talked with him for almost an hour before I could finally muster the courage to admit that the Sunday before I had chosen to be in sin instead of in the sanctuary. When I did, it became one of the first tastes of water from that living spring. I had convinced myself that my sin would cast me off from the place that I was starting to call home. For it is so easy for me to believe the grace of Christ can cover all sins but mine. But instead I was given grace. The type that Jesus says will mark us as His people. The type that made Jesus attractive to the notorious sinners that always seemed to know both where Jesus was and where the after party was being held. Which often seemed to be a place that Jesus was too.

I understand that when many people go through seasons of brokenness they don't turn to broken wells. They suffer through it much better than I had done/am doing. But I also understand that I am not alone in trying to dig wells to quench the thirst that only Jesus can truly satisfy.

I hope that through this season that you are able to find people whom you trust and confide in them. Tell them of your own broken wells. I have found that often when we turn to people and confess our sins that the dam of grace begins to break and cover us from head to toe. But we'll get to more of that later on and at a greater length.

Another well that I dug for myself was the well of pornography. Damn, writing that I still feel the need to hide myself. I am scared that many of you will put this book down and go no further. I'm scared that reading that confession will make you look at me different. But I also know that many of you will be able to say, "Damn, me too."

When I was younger I had a short-lived season in MMA. Though, I am still undefeated. I retired young at 3-0. But while I was training a lot a guy joined our gym. I liked him when we trained together, and I love him now.

I'm a smaller guy. I weighed myself today with my clothes on and weighted a whopping 133lbs. And my friend, Malcolm, probably has that much weight in one leg. He stands at least a foot taller than I do and his muscles have muscles. Once we went to grab a drink and catch up, some people simply assumed that we sold drugs because I came from work where I had to be decently dressed and he came from the gym. Me, a small white guy dressed well and him a towering African-American guy in gym clothes. But we weren't selling drugs. I haven't been an herbal distributionist since high school, and even then I wasn't that good of one. I never really learned that you shouldn't get high on your own supply.

Before we go any further, I have to let you know something. Mostly because including this will make my dear friend laugh. Almost expecting it to be here.

Back when Malcolm and I trained MMA I beat him up. Although I am not signing up for a rematch now that he has learned how to wrestle and I haven't trained in quite some time. I like my 'retired' record of having beaten him and don't want to lose it with a rematch now.

While I was living out in Oregon, Malcolm had become a Christian, though I didn't know it. One day after I moved home I was walking through downtown Auburn, AL and he ran up to me. We had lost contact with each other when I moved and here he was. For some reason still living in a college town as old as I was.

As we caught up he told me how Christ had brought him into the Family. And the more we hung out the closer we got.

Then one time, as we were spending time together he kept starting to say something and then holding it back. This happened a few times until finally I spoke for him.

"You want to confess looking at porn."

"Yea..."

"Honestly man, I have to as well."

In that moment, we both braced for the condemnation that we knew would follow. For is not porn the boldest scarlet letter of the Church? Is it not the only sin, save homosexuality (and honesty), that we believe will cast us out of the camp? Other sins get a wink or a blind eye. Pride turned the devil into the devil, and we have come to expect it in out 'best' preachers. Jesus spoke pretty hard about divorce being adultery, and we have all but swept that under the rug[4].

We had both dug the same well, and though confession we each found someone to help us go back and fill it in.

But to fill in a broken well seems to be much harder than digging it in the first place.

As I mentioned in the opening of this chapter, in high school I had once become so thirsty that I had drank warm shower water. A pound of it. But that story didn't end there. My wrestling coaches in high school weren't the best. But I was able to, more or less, wrestle year round and that was because I had older guys who seemed happy to help train me. My older brother, Andy Roberts, Trey Hammer, Justin Taylor, and Wade Preston more than any others.

---

[4] If you have been divorced, please know there is grace for every sin. Each and every one. Christ died for ALL the sins of ALL His people. And if this is the reason for your brokenness please continue to read. I could never be the one to condemn, for my life is a story of Christ covering a multitude of sin.

I remember telling one of them, who at the time was a Junior at Auburn University, if I remember right, and he had a solution. He gave me a can of chew, which is smokeless tobacco for those of ya'll who might not know that. He told me that if I had a pinch of this in my lip while I took a shower I would never drink the water that found its way into my mouth. Which led to me dipping on and off for the better part of 8 years. I still use tobacco everyday, but it's recently been a rotation between Sockeye's Bulls Eye Blend and a really nice Navy Flake in one of my pipes.

And in some ways, filling up a broken well means we need something that will keep us from drinking its water. We need something that would make drinking what finds its way across out lips as disgusting as drinking dip spit. In other words we can't simply not want to sin, we have to get to the place where we both hate and fight it.

We drink from other wells, and like a 16 year old boy who just became a pound overweight the night before a rival dual match we become frantic. I'm not sure if you're a believer in Christ. I have no way of knowing that. And even if I knew you I could be fooled. One of the people I though I knew best in my life fooled me, and many others on that front. And I'm sure you could too. But I would challenge you to wrestle with it. For, after all, we are each called to work out our own salvation with fear and trembling[5].

So where do we run to when we find ourselves thirsty with only dirt water to drink?

Look back at that passage from Jeremiah.

---

[5] Philippians 2:12

"for my people have committed two evils;
they have forsaken me,
the fountain of living waters,
and hewed out for themselves,
broken cisterns that can hold no water."

God was calling out His people for turning to their broken wells but we read that doing so was only one of two sins they had committed. The other was that they had turned from Him, the only fountain of living water.

So it seems that turning from the broken wells that we have made for ourselves is only part of the answer, just as going to them was only part of the problem. We must once again return to Him who is the fountain. For it is only here that we can be truly satisfied. It is only once we return to that fountain that we shall be able to drink our fill and be truly satisfied.

But in doing so we must confess that somewhere down the line there was a shift in our hearts. For each of us who has made a broken well, there was first a belief that God could not, or would not, satisfy us any longer. We get to the place where we don't believe that what God has to offer us is good, because we have stopped believing that God is good.

In looking for living water we could also look to the story of the woman at the well in John 4. The one where Jesus met a woman wanting something to drink, and instead Jesus gave her Himself. Not a theological premise of who He is as the Messiah. He gives her His love and acceptance. But I'm getting ahead of myself, as we shall venture there a little further on.

And it's here that I begin to see another broken well that I had been drinking from. The one I described as a spring, the one that I went to and upon finding dry turned to all the others.

I have come to believe that everyone is a nerd in once sense or another. And in a lot of ways I am a theological nerd. To prove the point I think that a 700 page book on the theological implications of direct atonement is going to be a fun read and I keep seminary classes from Reformed Theological Seminary in my podcast lineup.

And because of that I can get pretty heady when it comes to my understanding of God. Which I don't think is a bad thing in itself, but it can easily become a substitute for knowing God. And often when that happens people turn into jerks. At least that happened to me. It's why people often jokingly use the term 'cage stage' for someone who has newly become a Calvinist.

Through my pursuit of a theological knowledge I had, without knowing it, placed God in a folder marked Theology. And each time I ran to it I opened up the pages of information looking for something to satisfy me. What I was doing could be compared to a wife reciting facts about her husband after a fight when all he asked was that she come to bed.

But through my broken-heartedness I saw the broken heart of my Abba. Through Jeremiah He was calling out that He was all that was needed to live. He was offering me that which would truly satisfy as He watched me chasing after my broken wells. And yet the people that He had called His own, and the people that called Him their own, turned to other, easier, things. And I had followed their example of brokenness.

It was in this season of dryness and brokenness that I first arrived at the place where I understood the difference between wanting to pray and needing to pray. It was here in this season of being broken and dry that I came to understand that though I knew quite a bit about God I did not know Him as nearly much as I once believed I had.

There had been times where I prayed until I was hoarse. Times when I had given it my all. I served my King, Jesus. I knew that God was my Father. But there was something missing. I theologically understood the doctrine of adoption but I went through life as if I was anything but His true son. And it was this season of brokenness that showed me that.

My dad has become one of my best friends. Honestly if I could only go to one person for advice, it would be my father. But we have had a rocky relationship. We have yelled at each other, more me than him. We've gone far too long with out speaking, again probably my fault; definitely my fault.

My father is one of the best, if not the best, man that I know. And I know all of his faults. But there is something that you need to know. When I talk to other people…when I write now about him, I will call him either 'my dad' or 'my father'. But that's not what I call him. Honestly if I ever called him either of those things he would likely ask me what was wrong. When I call him, I call him 'pops'. It's a name that has come to be intimate. I could yell it across a crowded room and he would respond. He would know it was me, because it's a name that was born of intimacy. The same way that I still call my mother 'momma' and will do till we're both gone to Canaan's shore. And maybe after that as well…

Before this season of brokenness, this season of dry desperation, I was ok with calling God by a name less intimate. And honestly, I was annoyed when people didn't do the same. I had mistaken their intimacy for irreverence.

When Jesus taught us, His little brothers and sisters, to pray He told us to call His Father by an intimate name. Abba. Right now as you read this I would invite you to join me in a borrowed prayer from a broken hero.

"Abba, I belong to You.[6]"

It's a quick prayer. One that I have come to pray often. It's short enough to pray while walking a hall between rooms at work. Before we finish I would invite you to place this book down and pray it. Pray it 5, 10, or 20 times. Pray it until it feels like a true statement.

That's the spring of water I was looking for. And whether you know it or not, it's the spring which you have been searching for as well. Because, I believe, our adoption by the Father is the hinge-point of our entire faith. For it is when we are able to see God the Father as someone who loves us that we are able to see the water He gives as something we need, and something that we want. As long as we view the Father as distant, angry with us, wanting us to be better before we can be loved, or standing ready to punish us each time we don't make a perfect score; we shall never be able to run to Him to be satisfied. Until we understand that we can call Him Abba we shall never give up our broken well in exchange for living water.

It's not an easy thing to do. But then again, Jesus never said it would be. In fact He promises trouble[7]. But Jesus, through every temptation to go to a broken well, knew who He was. And who He was, and still is, is rooted in who Abba is and who He is in relation to Abba.

---

[6] This is a short prayer that Brennan Manning would invite people to pray.
[7] John 16:33

It's easy to come to a place where we have a proper theological view of God in almost every way, but miss His love for us. We point to the cross. And that truly is one of, if not the foremost, points of contact between God's love and our brokenness. But it is not the only one. For the cross is lost of its beauty when we forget what was purchased there.

LUX

PRAYER:

Abba,
You are good beyond all thought,
But I am sinful, wretched, broken, and blind;
My lips want to confess what I have done,
But my heart is so slow to feel,
And I am slow to change what I am doing.
I bring all of me to You; my heart, my mind, my strength, my Soul,
break it, wound it, bend it, mould it.
Give me the strength to take off my mask,
And show me my sin,
That I may hate my sin, be repulsed by my sin, and run from My Sin.
My own self has been a tool and weapon against you,
As a rebel I have misused the strength you have given me,
And served the foul enemy of your kingdom and my own fFesh.
Give me grace to lament my numbed recklessness.
Let me understand that the road of sin is hard and painful,
That sinful paths are wretched paths,
And that to run from You is to lose all good.
I have seen the purity and the beauty of Your perfect law,
The happiness of those who truly know Your love,
The calm majesty of the path You walk on,
And the majesty of those who follow You on that path,
But still I daily find myself running from you.
But the Holy Spirit, full of love, wrestles with me,
He brings to mind what Scripture has called me to,
He speaks through Your Word, by the family you have given,
He points me back to you through providence,
He calls me sweetly and gently back to You.

Yet I so often choose things that only end up hurting me
More.
Things that hurt and grieve Your heart as well.
Abba, I hate these sins that are within me.
Teach me to hate them more. Teach me to cry for mercy and
Grace.
Give me the strength to turn to you again in true repentance,
Teach me the secret of true grief of my sins.
Teach me godly grief,
Grief that trembles and fears, yet ever trusts and loves You.
Grief that leads back to powerful confidence in You.
Let me, through honest tears of repentance,
See clearly the brightness, goodness, and glories of the
Saving Cross.
Teach me to ever be running to it, till at last I finish running.[8]

---

[8] Adapted from 'Yet I Sin' in the Valley of Vision Prayer Book.

V
Unanswered prayers

"How long, O LORD? Will you forget me forever? How long will you hide your face from me? How long must I take counsel in my soul and have sorrow in my heart all the day? How long shall my enemy be exalted over me? Consider and answer me, O LORD my God; light up my eyes, lest I sleep the sleep of death" –Psalm 13:1-3

"He who counts the stars, and calls them by their names is in no danger of forgetting His own children." –Charles Spurgeon

I can still remember sitting in my parents living room almost two years ago now and trying to figure out what to do with all the shattered pieces of my life. And trying to tell myself that I was not as broken as it seemed in that moment. Trying to ignore the truth, that not only was I that broken…but far more so. All that I had hoped for and trusted in has collapsed upon me.

In reading that I know that some of you know the feeling. And for those of you who don't, I hope you never have to. But chances are that you will. And when that happens, I hope that somehow God can use this story of my brokenness to help you through your own season of the same.

When Christ talks of fasting He speaks of it in a way that He assumes that His followers would do it[1]. He took it as a simple fact that it would be a natural rhythm in the life of those who would be called by His name. And for me I have always been told, and seen, fasting as an act of desperation. It was a coming to terms that we can do nothing, and God must be the one who acts. It is a way of saying that an answer from God is more valuable than the food we are giving up. Maybe that's why we in the West do it so seldom, for we so seldom

---

[1] Matthew 6:16

feel desperate. But I had gotten to a place of desperation. I had gotten to the place where I knew that it had to be God who acted. And so I decided that I would take time to pray and fast. And I did, longer than I ever had before. I spent longer that I thought I could without food, cried so much I thought I would become dehydrated, and prayed myself hoarse.

As I have stated previously, the spark that burned started the wildfire that would come to consume me was a broken engagement. I spent that summer trying to make things work out any way that I could. At the end of the summer I was scheduled to lead a mission trip to Mexico for the church I had been working with in Oregon[2]. I spent that last week before the trip fasting and praying. And on the drive down to Mexico the decision was made that me and her not talk the week I was in Texas/Mexico so that we could each pray, and also so that I could focus on the team I was leading.

When leading these trips I can almost go on autopilot. I have been on more than I can say and have led a good number as well. So as much as I didn't want to, I went on autopilot. Other than my little sister, Blake, and Andrew I kept myself aloof and in prayer. While on the trip we always stay in Texas and cross the boarder into Mexico each morning and then cross back into Texas each afternoon.

I got there early on a Saturday morning and then picked up the team later that afternoon. The next day we went to Logos Community Church[3] in McAllen, TX and then to a street market in Progresso, Mexico. While walking around the market I looked at rings. I wear a few and have lost more

---

[2] If you'd ever like to come on a mission trip with me go to www.harvestevangelism.org and let me know. I'd love to take you down.
[3] www.logoscommunity.com

than a gypsy has owned. In one shop I saw a ring that would be perfect, perfect for my own wedding band. So I went ahead and bought it. A fact that, until the words were upon this page, only my sister, myself, and God knew. But I bought it. Because I *knew* that God was going to answer my prayer and fasting. I *knew* that He was going to do this for me. I *knew* He was going to work it out. I have seen Him answer other prayers. And I had never prayed harder for anything else in my life. And this was an act of my faith, for I '*knew*' what the answer would be.

Each day I would wear the ring on my right hand as a reminder to pray even more, and at night I would sleep with it on my left as I have mentioned earlier in this book.

A week later I was on my parent's couch and that ring was somewhere in the gutters of Downtown Opelika, AL. At least that's where I threw it. Sitting there my mother, speaking as sweetly as she could, reminded me that there is a song about unanswered prayers. I'm sure you know it. I'm not much of a Garth Brooks fan, but everyone knows that song. That one, and Friends in Low Places. "Sometimes I thank God for unanswered prayers." At least according to Mr. Brooks.

I'm happy for Garth. But I wasn't at a place where I could say that. And still not always at a place where I can, though I can agree with him slightly more often than I disagree these days. And that's the way we want to look at such things. We want to be able to sing along and mean the words as if they were a hymn sung on Sunday. But honestly, sometimes those aren't sung with pure conviction either.

When these things happen we begin to ask the types of questions that we thought we never would. For me I truly believed that God had told me that this was the girl I was going to marry. I fully believed it. And so I was left with to questions that lurked over me like a raincloud that follows you on a road trip through the Great Plains. “Did God lie to me?” or “Do I not hear Him at all?” And both of those questions were worse than the other.

If you are at a place where those are the questions that are running around your head at the moment, I would beg you to press on. At least thought the end of this chapter.

In his book titled simply, *Prayer*, Richard Foster writes of Jesus the night before He was murdered, “Here we have the incarnate Son praying through his tears and not receiving what he asks. Jesus knew the burden of unanswered prayer. ‘If you are willing,’ was his question, his wondering. The Father’s will was not yet absolutely clear to him. ‘Is there any other way?’ ‘Can people be redeemed by some other means?’ The answer—no! Andrew Murry writes, ‘For our sins, He suffered beneath the burden of that unanswered prayer.’…But in the school of Gethsemane we learn to distrust whatever is of our own mind, thought, and will even though it is not directly sinful. Jesus shows us a more excellent way. The way of helplessness. The way of abandonment. The way of relinquishment. ‘My will be done’ is conquered by ‘not my will.’”

Here Foster gets right to where we must go. Right where I was. To the question of prayers unanswered. But he also shows us that we are not alone in praying them. Which is something I needed to hear, and if you are reading this book, it is something that I can only assume that you need as well.

Jesus was met with an unanswered prayer and yet landed in trusting His Father’s will over His momentary desires. But when my prayers went unanswered I looked nothing like Jesus. Instead I ran away from the Father. I ran away from God, because if He was not going to answer I would find another god who would. I would run to something else to comfort me, something else to be there, something, anything that would not be silent. But in running to those idols of my own making, those false gods who promised more and delivered less, I found myself even emptier than I had been before. Though I thought I could never have been emptier than I was before.

And this prayer to be married was not the only unanswered prayer I have prayed through this dark season. I wrote in my journal as recent as this week that it often feels like each time I am able to get back on my feet the wind is knocked out of me once again. I have even lamented that it often feels like when I pray for other people God answers, and when I pray for myself He gives in return yet another unanswered prayer.

I have often returned to the parable of Jesus when He compared prayer to a widow annoying the local judge[4]. She persisted and got what she asked for. And Jesus told us to pray like that, to keep coming back. That no matter what happened we should 'pray through'. And yet, I often feel as though I have done all that I could to pray through and yet remained with prayers unanswered. So when this is the place that we get to, what do we do? For if you are anything like me, it is tempting to simply give up what little faith is left and throw in the towel. For Jesus promised a load that would be light and a burden that would not break us. So what shall we do when the burden stays heavy and we must admit to being broken?

Tonight I sat with 6 or 7 other people for the first bible study of has become Union Church[5], the small little church plant that I stayed in Alabama for after moving back from Oregon, and we spoke of life in the flesh vs life in Christ. What does each offer us. When speaking of life in the flesh we said that

---

[4] Luke 18:1-8
[5] www.unionchurchao.com

one of the many things that would be produced would be pain. And for each item listed in that column labeled 'flesh' there was something clearly different that was given under the column labeled 'Christ'. In return for brokenness in the flesh we can receive healing in Christ. Where the flesh will push us into isolation life, in Christ is accompanied with true communion both with God and with others through the local church. But when we got to pain it was different. When we got there we did not say that we would be given all that is promised by preachers with cheap words and expensive smiles. We spoke of how in Christ we are not given a 'get out of pain free' card. We are given Christ. The one who knows our pain, our weakness, our fear, and our grief over unanswered prayers. In Christ we are given one who has walked this path before us and can lead us safely through.

I prayed and prayed that I would be married to that girl. But while writing this I am still single and it looks like she might marry someone I once called a friend instead of me. I can hear Garth singing in the background, and sometimes still, I think he might just be full of it. It seems easy for him to sing such a song. Showing up at an old reunion and running into an old fling, but being accompanied by someone he now loved. I wonder if he would have written the same song had he showed up alone? Would he have one less hit song that people bought tickets to sing along to[6]?

Because if we are honest, unanswered prayers have a way of seeping into our bones and shaping much of who we are. "If only…" we tell ourselves. We begin to look at everything that could be and all that is not and believe that if God had only given us this, or answered us then, all would be different. Maybe the night would not be as dark. Maybe the darkness would not be lasting so long. We look to all these

[6] Does he still tour? I really don't know, and don't feel troubled to look it up.

things that we believe would save us, and then blame God for our lack of salvation. But this is where we can begin to see what God may be doing through prayers left unanswered.

It's easy for me to look at the unanswered prayers of others and have full faith that God will show up and show out. But when looking at my own, what I truly felt and I'm sure that many of you feel now is the anger, pain, and loneliness that so often comes when ours prayers don't seem to get past the ceiling. If only I had this thing that God could easily give, I often catch myself thinking, then I would be satisfied. But in thinking this way we begin to see God more like the genie from *Aladdin* than who He truly is. Thinking we can trick Him to get us out of the Cave of Wonders without wasting a wish. We see, at least I can, that though there is a hatred of seeing God in such a way we often do just that. I have done just that. I believed that God owed me this one. This prayer was owed to me. I may have directed my prayers to God, but I centered them around myself.

With each prayer unanswered, and I still have a few, there is a pain that follows. But so often we try to cover up these feeling. Because so often these feelings are not welcomed in the church anymore, people there seem to only want honesty when life is treating us well. If only we had more faith, we think, these prayers would be answered. Or from the other side of the isle we think that if we just trusted God more these things wouldn't hurt so bad—insert Romans 8:28 out of context, and just be ok again.

But we need only look back to that unanswered prayer of Christ. Dare we say He lacked faith? Would we claim that He had a bad theology or lack of trust in His Father? Not at all. Yet He prays an unanswered prayer, and is driven to the point of pain, turmoil, and stress that causes His blood vessels to rupture[7]. In the end, Jesus resolved that He would place Himself in His Father's hands. In His Father's will. And in doing so, He calls us to do the same.

In my unanswered prayers I have seen that, when I continue to press into God through prayer, worship, and community, I begin to see something. I had looked to God to give me these things, good things as far as the Scripture is concerned, as a road to fulfillment. I had wanted God to give me the things that would in the end be my demise. Then I called Him a bad Father for not giving them. For when we look to something to give us contentment and fulfillment, that thing becomes our functional god. And only the true God of the Bible can bear that weight for any amount of time and not come crashing down upon us.

And I have seen the gods I made for myself crumble under that weight more than once.

In the wake of unanswered prayers we have a plethora[8] of questions like the ones I mentioned above. Another question that comes to the surface for all of us who are honest enough to admit it is, "Where are you God?" For when prayers go unanswered they often feel as though they are prayers unheard. But one thing that I have found is that, though this season of darkness, fear, depression, and all else that can be connected to a 'Dark Night of the Soul', is that I have found God to be closer that I though He was before I first cried out asking where He had gone. For often times prayers unanswered are there to mend relationship un-had.

---

[7] https://www.medicalnewstoday.com/articles/319110.php

[8] This has been one of my favorite words since I first heard it spoken by El Guapo in the movie The Three Amigos. I still say it in my head in this horrible Mexican accent.

I can't speak into your experience, but I can speak from mine. And I can assume that though the reasons for our darkness may differ, our darkness may not. And it was within the darkest of nights that I began to see that all the lamps I had lit for myself, one-by-one, go dark. It was in this season that the markers I had set for my life and the path I had laid out for myself turned to dust. And it was in this season that I finally gave up and allowed God to lead me. Or at least I am trying to. And lead me He has. He did not lead me to a place that is happy or easy. He has led me to the place where Christ was. He led me to a place of death and resurrection. And just like so many, I wanted resurrection pleasure without Golgotha pain. If that was available to any, it would have been available to Christ. Yet so often we believe that it is somehow something which we have earned or are owed. Though we wouldn't admit it.

Two and a half years ago I would have, with full assurance, told you that Jesus was my only God. But in all honesty our functional god is the thing that we could not live without. And when I was left with only Jesus I didn't want to live anymore. And though it was painful, God took away everything that I had allowed to function as my god. He allowed it to fall under the weight of the idols I had erected in my heart. And in doing so He broke me. But He broke me to save me. He wounded me to heal me.

It was through the wreck of my unanswered prayers that I began to learn how to press into God harder than I had ever done before. And it was in this season that He became as dear to me as I had claimed He had been before this all began. So I would invite you to do the same. See the prayers that seem to have fallen on deaf ears as an answer in themselves. Pray that you may begin to see having God as a better thing than having the things which He could give you, or give back to you. These things that you think will give you true comfort, ease, satisfaction, or joy will do nothing but destroy you. As hard as it is to admit, we must remember that in this season we must make our bed at the Throne of Grace and beg for the faith to even pray again. I have been there. I have prayed till I had nothing left and then gone to bed empty. And I have, at times, begged and received nothing more than the strength to do the same thing again.

But there are other times. Times that make all the rest worth the struggle. Times that make the fighting worth the beating taken. For joy that is fought for is so much sweeter than joy that comes easy. When it cost us everything, then, and only then, it can truly be everything.

There is a verse that I have memorized and come back to often. "Delight yourself in the LORD, and He will give you the desires of your heart.[9]" It's a verse that I'm sure you know or have at least heard before. When I first entered this season, a season that I am still in, that I prayed out:

"God I have delighted myself in You, so what's going on? You're not holding up Your side of this deal!"

If you are in this season as well then I'm sure you've uttered the same words, or at least something similar. I am certain that you have felt as if God owed you one, as if He was a co-worker that agreed to cover a shift since you did the same. But as I have begun to see more and more of my own heart, I see more and more that I wanted God to give me what I believed would satisfy me instead of believing that He could satisfy me. I have seen that in doing so I was not truly delighting myself in Him, only in that which He gave. I was simply delighted that I believed He would give me what I really wanted. I have continued to weave this verse into my

---

[9] Psalm 37:4

prayer but much more I ask God to teach me to truly delight in Him. I'm not there yet, and I'm not even sure if I'll ever fully get there. I still ask that He would grant some of these prayers, that He would grant these things that my heart desires. But I also ask that if these desires are not from Him, that He would give me the grace of changing what I desire.

And though it is not easy. Through a long season of unanswered prayer I have learned to truly pray. To pray though my doubts and fears, which is often for they seem to come back each day like the tide. I have learned to trust God more for who He is than for what He can give. And I would invite you to do the same. Find time to pray when it's just you and your Abba, and time when the family that your Abba has adopted you into joins you. Press into prayer and ask the Holy Spirit to teach you to pray. Press in and ask that God would show you that He truly is a good, good Father. And that such a phrase is more than just a line in a popular worship song.

Doing this has not been easy for me. Even tonight before writing this I walked around the little downtown where I live and prayed. And while praying I came to all the places where I still doubt, all the places where unanswered prayers lie that God does not hear or cannot act. But in prayer I come to find the faith that only prayer can give us. For we have a Father who does hear us and act for our true good. And we return again to Jesus telling us to be like that widow[10]. To come back again, and come back after that. That some things are only given after we beat down the door for longer than we think we should have to. And when we do, we find that we are given what we needed instead of what we wanted. Like a little child crying for more candy and being given a proper dinner.

---

[10] Luke 18:1-8

When this happens we will be able to truly appreciate what we have been given. And we shall be able to see past the gifts that we have been given to the loving God who gives them. Which will keep us, at least for a season, from making gods out of our gifts and starting the cycle all over again.

So maybe, just maybe, I agree with Garth a little more than I would admit to. And I pray that you will be able to do the same. Either way I would invite you to pray with me. God can hear even the silent prayers that we pray, but sometimes we need to be able to hear ourselves. So pray this one aloud. Sometimes in prayer we must speak not only to God, but to our own soul.

PRAYER:

Abba,
Fill me with Your Spirit and teach me to pray.
I confess that often when I come to You in prayer,
The words I say and what I believe are at odds.
I have often treated prayer so carelessly.
I so flippantly that those in heaven would be shocked.
I have desired thing which would have only hurt me,
And when you keep me from harm I become angry with You.
I have viewed the mercy you give as nothing of value.
I have allowed both my hopes and my fears
To cause me to doubt that You are a good Father.
Lord, I admit that I am truly unfit to choose for myself,
For when I follow my own heart I am lead into trouble.
Please allow Your Spirit to help me where I fall short,
For I know that I don't even pray in the ways that I should.
Place in my heart only those desires which You have for me.
Teach me to pray for that which is for my good,
And Your glory.
When You do I will have full confidence
That You have heard me.
Lead me to the place where I desire You above all,
More than any blessing that You could or will give me.
Let me remember that You know all that I need,
Even before I ask You for it.
Never let me believe the lie that I have all that I need,
Unless I have You fully and completely.
Never let me be satisfied outside of Your presence.
Never allow me to believe that I know all in times
When I am far from You.

Let me seek, above all else, Your Kingdom.
Let my greatest value be placed on things that are eternal.
Let me be poor, afflicted, despised and be at Your side,
Rather than have all the world can offer me
And be far from You.
Let me not forget that You are better than and success,
Better than any wish I could wish for,
Better than being loved and accepted by any or by all.
Don't let me forget that this world is but a dream,
Give me the faith to desire my true home with You.
And let that be what I long for above all.
Let me always seek my happiness in Your favor,
Your image, Your presence, and Your service.[11]

---

[11] Adapted from 'Desires' in The Valley of Vision Prayer Book

VI
Homeward Bound

"For we know that if the tent that is our earthly home is destroyed, we have a building from God, a house not made with hands, eternal in the heavens. For in this tent we groan, longing to put on our heavenly dwelling, if indeed by putting it on we may not be found naked. For while we are still in this tent, we groan, being burdened—not that we would be unclothed, but that we would be further clothed, so that what is mortal may be swallowed up by life. He who has prepared us for this very thing is God, who has given us the Spirit as a guarantee."
-2 Corinthians 5:1-5

"God knows very well what we need and that all he does if for our good. If knew how much He loves us, we would always be ready to face life itself—both its pleasures and its troubles."
–Brother Lawrence

"Is this what Christianity is?
We promise people joy without having it, and just wait for Heaven.
If that's all it is, I'm done.
Honesty, if that's all it is, I kinda just want to die."

I have uttered the same questions. And I have even arrived at the same conclusion more than I would like to admit. But to hear it from another voice, one with the type of pain that I have felt in the past, caused me to feel it anew and see it differently.

It was odd; when I heard this question from someone who was just as broken as I have often been, my first inclination was to give all the churchy answers that I've grown to hate. They type that I have already talked about. I wanted to offer up a 'silver bullet' that would till at that was bad and make everything ok again. Even after knowing how much I hated when people offered this to me, my knee-jerk reaction was to give him the very thing I wished people had never given to me. I wanted to do what so many had tried to do for me, I wanted to tell him the 'right thing' that would make everything ok. Or to say it a more honest way, I wanted to fix him. As if I have forgotten that every time I have tried to fix others, or myself for that matter, the result was often destruction. But even as those words swelled around my head I came to hate them. For I knew that random verses and promises seemingly built upon sand cannot stand, even a single night, in the middle of a storm.

A few years back I was sitting at my parent's house with my momma and her sister. As we sat there my mom got a phone call. One of those life-will-never-be-the-same type of calls. We ran to her car and drove across town to where one of our family friends lived. Or I guess I should say where he had lived. Because even though we showed up before they took his body, he hadn't been there since the night before.

In the midst of a suicide there are always questions that are asked, on both sides of the gun. The type of questions that I hope you have never had to wrestle with, but the type of questions I believe that a lot of you have. Lord knows I have asked them on both sides more than once.

This guy had gone through seminary. He had preached in my church back when I was a pastor. He was like a son to my father; having traveled the world with him on various mission trips. He had preached sermons on the very issues that seemingly had defeated him. I can remember my mom asking me how could it be that he didn't trust what he knew, what he had preached? But in a twisted way, I believe he did. In the darkness he found himself, maybe it was that he trusted certain truths more than he ever had. For there is a truth, for the Christian, that once this life ends we will enter into joy everlasting. A truth that though this life is hard, once it is over we will live a life void of pain, hurt, and heartbreak.

And as with many truths, the enemy can twist it six ways from Sunday. The truth that there is a hope of the next life twists to a voice saying to go there now. That the beauty of what is to come begins to overshadow any joy or hope that is still in the here and now. I can only assume. But I can assume, because those twisted truths have rambled in my head more than once.

For many this may sound odd, and for some of you it will resonate deeply. And if that is you, I am truly sorry. But I think that why most of us find this so odd is because in our culture we have no real idea of what Heaven will be like, or the New Jerusalem after it[1]. We have bookshelves full of Christian best sellers that describe Heaven, but they seem to be rooted more in our own fantasy than the holy words of Scripture. We are a people who have been sold a bill-of-goods about what heaven is. We imaging floating clouds full of naked babies playing the harp. And that's not somewhere I really want to go. I'm not even sure I'd be allowed around all those naked babies as a single guy with a mustache who's pushing 30. And I think because of that idea; so many of us have not listened to Jesus when He said that where our treasure is, there our heart will be also[2]. But, sadly, many in the faith don't long for Home at all, because many of us will arrive there to find ourselves poor in a place that promises riches. Having stored up all our treasure in a place where moth can destroy and a thief can come and steal[3].

We have become a people that view religion as a box to check on Sunday mornings, and, if we are good, for five minuets each morning. But the way that Scripture talks about

---

[1] Biblically speaking Heaven is not our home. For even Heaven itself will be destroyed and made new. For those of us who are in Christ our eternal home will be the New Jerusalem on the New Earth.

[2] Matthew 6:21

[3] Matthew 6:20

Home is so much better than these small boxes could ever allow us to imagine. It's a place to be longed for…

In the last book of the bible, near the end, St. John gives us a picture of what it'll be like.

"Then I saw a new heaven and a new earth, for the first heaven and the first earth had passed away, and the sea was no more. And I saw the holy city, New Jerusalem, coming down out of heaven from God, prepared as a bride adorned for her husband. And I heard a loud voice from the throne saying, 'Behold, the dwelling place of God is with man. He will dwell with them, and they will be his people, and God himself will be with them as their God. He will wipe away every tear from their eyes, and death shall be no more, neither shall there be mourning, nor crying, nor pain anymore, for the former things have passed away.'

And he who was seated on the throne said, 'Behold, I am making all things new.' Also he said, 'Write this down, for these words are trustworthy and true.' And he said to me, 'It is done! I am the Alpha and the Omega, the beginning and the end. To the thirsty I will give from the spring of the water of life without payment. The one who conquers will have this heritage, and I will be his God and he will be my son. But as for the cowardly, the faithless, the detestable, as for murderers, the sexually immoral, sorcerers, idolaters, and all liars, their portion will be in the lake that burns with fire and sulfur, which is the second death.'

Then came one of the seven angels who had the seven bowls full of the seven last plagues and spoke to me, saying, 'Come, I will show you the Bride, the wife of the Lamb.' And he carried me away in the Spirit to a great, high mountain, and showed me the holy city Jerusalem coming down out of heaven from God, having the glory of God, its radiance like a most rare jewel, like a jasper, clear as crystal. It had a great, high wall, with twelve gates, and at the gates twelve angels, and on the gates the names of the twelve tribes of the sons of Israel were inscribed— on the east three gates, on the north three gates, on the south three gates, and on the west three gates. And the wall of the city had twelve foundations, and on them were the twelve names of the twelve apostles of the Lamb.

And the one who spoke with me had a measuring rod of gold to measure the city and its gates and walls. The city lies foursquare, its length the same as its width. And he measured the city with his rod, 12,000 stadia. Its length and width and height are equal. He also measured its wall, 144 cubits by human measurement, which is also an angel's measurement. The wall was built of jasper, while the city was pure gold, like clear glass. The foundations of the wall of the city were adorned with every kind of jewel. The first was jasper, the second sapphire, the third agate, the fourth emerald, the fifth onyx, the sixth carnelian, the seventh chrysolite, the eighth beryl, the ninth topaz, the tenth chrysoprase, the eleventh jacinth, the twelfth amethyst. And the twelve gates were twelve pearls, each of the gates made of a single pearl, and the street of the city was pure gold, like transparent glass.

And I saw no temple in the city, for its temple is the Lord God the Almighty and the Lamb. And the city has no need of sun or moon to shine on it, for the glory of God gives it light, and its lamp is the Lamb. By its light will the nations walk, and the kings of the earth will bring their glory into it, and its gates will never be shut by day—and there will be no night there. They will bring into it the glory and the honor of the nations. But nothing unclean will ever enter it, nor anyone who does what is detestable or false, but only those who are written in the Lamb's book of life.[4]"

I'm not sure about you. But for me, that sounds a lot better than anything here. Just imagine it for a moment. A city that has no need of police, or police reform. A city where there is

---

[4] Revelation 21

no one who dies because it's too cold to be sleeping on the streets. A city where there is no one sleeping on the streets. A city where kids don't go to school just so that they can eat once a day. A city where there is no mourning because there is no sin to be mourned. Neither our own sin that keeps us up at night nor the sins of others that seem to have cut so deep that the wounds may never heal. A city where Jesus is right there with us; to be grabbed, and hugged, and hold onto. A city that has no need of lights; because God, in all His glory, will be that close to us. Always. A city that will make Sinai look like a cheesy Thomas Kincaid rendering of glory.

If you're anything like me, this almost sounds too good to be true. But still, there is something in these words that seem to draw us Home. At least that is what happens when I read them. They seem as comforting as good corned-beef and cabbage cooked just right on momma's table. Because there is something in these words that both seem like home, and call us there at the same time. And yet, we know that what we have read is something that we have never seem or felt. It's a desire that we hold in us that this world can't seem to fill. But as C.S. Lewis once said, "If I find in myself desires which nothing in this world can satisfy, the only logical explanation is that I was made for another world.[5]" So even in this we find that we were made for a world that isn't broken. And maybe, just maybe, God has allowed us to feel the brokenness of this world as a not-so-subtle reminder that this isn't home. Maybe even our pain is a reminder that we are not yet at our destination.

But when we get here, to the understanding of what Home will be like, the pain of this world can seem even greater. It's like that anticipation you feel on the last leg of a trip.

---

[5] Lewis, C. S. (1960). Christian Behavior: Hope. In *Mere Christianity*(p. 120). New York, NY: MacMillian Publishing Company.

Knowing that where you have been going is just a littler further up the road. And when you get there, you can get out of a messy car and walk around. You can see that the view outside the window begin to change and everything in you just wants to be where you are going. If you've never experienced this, all you have to do is road trip out to the Rockies. The mountains will stand in the distance for what seems like forever and yet all you seem to drive through is the cornfield that is Kansas. You can see the place you want to be, even at times feel the cold air pushed down from the peaks. But all you have around you is corn.

Within his book, *Finding Peace in Life's Storms*, Charles Spurgeon puts it like this:

"And so, our poor bodies are not well matched with our newborn souls, since they have not yet been born again. They are somewhat dull and dreary dwellings for heaven-born spirits! With their aches and pains; weariness and infirmity; need of sleep, food, and clothing; susceptibility to cold, heat, accident, and decay, as well as to excessive labor and exhausting toil, they are pitifully incapable of serving those who are sanctified…

Since sin dwells in our hearts and we are clothed in mortal clay, we are glad that our salvation is nearer to us now than when we first believed, and we long to enter into the full enjoyment of it. Scripture gives us a great amount of encouragement about this. There will come a time when we will be fully delivered from the cause of our present groaning. We will receive a salvation so wide that it will cover all of our needs and even all our desires. A salvation awaits us whose parameters are immense and eternal…We not only believe this, but we fervently desire it. *We desire it so much that, at times, we want to die so that we may enter into it.* All the time, but especially when we get a glimpse of Christ, our souls long to be with Him.

This desire is accompanied by confident expectation. We expect to see the glory of Christ and to share in it, as much as we expect to see tomorrow morning…We believe it, we desire it, and we expect it.[6]"

On more than one occasion I have prayed the same prayer, "Abba, I just want to go Home." It's a prayer that is two-fold. And if you have ever prayed this prayer then you understand what I mean by that. It's a prayer that says, "I just want to die. I want to be done will all of this pain, this regret, this shattered hope, this betrayal, this dark night." But it is also a prayer that has full assurance that once this life ends we will be with God forever, and that all that Scripture tells us of our true Home is true.

Before the dusk that led me into my dark night of the soul I would often pray that old prayer found at the very end of the book, "Maranatha[7]." But, honestly, I wanted Jesus to take His time. I wanted Him to come after I had gotten married. I wanted Him to come after I had enjoyed all the things I had seemingly been working for. I wanted Him to come back after I had gotten to live in the city again, after I had planted a church, after I had been able to be a father, after my check list was all checked off. But one of the things that happens when everything is taken away, is that we truly see what matters and what is valuable.

I had gotten to the place where I theologically believed that things would be better once I arrived at Canaan's shore. But I had a check-list of things that I needed Jesus to wait around

---

[6] Spurgeon, Charles H. "Saved In Hope." In *Finding Peace in Life's Storms*, 13-20. New Kensington, PA: Whitaker House, 1997. (Emphasis mine)

[7] 'Oh Lord, Come!' This is the word that St John used at the end of Revelation.

for me to accomplish. I never would have admitted it, and even writing this now I want to find a nicer, cleaner, churchier way to say this. Because I know that many of you will judge me for such a confession (or maybe not if you have gotten this far). And many of you that will do so, only will so you don't have to admit that you have felt the same way.

Once I arrived at the place where everything I had hoped to have, do, or accomplish was taken away from me. It seemed as if the only hope I had left was that once day I would be Home. To an elder place than Eden, and a taller town than Rome[8]. Suddenly it seemed as if the only thing left worth doing was getting to the end of the race. And more than once I figured that it was worth looking for a shortcut.

Maybe I am alone in thinking this, I doubt it, but who knows. I have often wished that I was already Home. Though I can look though scripture and see a lot of places where the promise of God is that I was made for good works which He prepared for me[9], or that He has a plan for my good[10], or that He decrees how long I'll live[11], and where I'll live[12]. I can see all of these things. But often I wish that I had drawn a different lot. At 28 there are a few people I've known who I can only see by looking at their name etched in stone. And there are times when I wish it were the other way around. I can look to all these promises of what Home will be like, and I wish that I was the one on that side of things looking back. I wish that I was covered in the glory of my Father instead of the brokenness of this world. I wish that I was in a place

---

[8] A description of Home taken from G.K. Chesterton's poem *The House of Christmas*
[9] Ephesians 2:10
[10] Jeremiah 29:11
[11] Job 14:5
[12] Acts 17:26

where my wounds no longer ached because I could physically cling to the wounds of Jesus. Although I know the truth, I can still hear it being twisted.

That is what my family friend heard. And in that moment when the gun cocked, I think that he believed more than he ever had that on the other side of a single decision was Home. And I think, in some way, he was right. I don't think that suicide is the unpardonable sin. No more so than being angry with someone and then dying in a car wreck before you repent is the unpardonable sin. As a good Calvinist, most of the time, I think that Jesus actually saved His people on the cross instead of just making their salvation possible. I trust Jesus when He said that all those that the Father gave Him will come to Him, and there is not one of those who will be lost[13]. For me that sounds like if Jesus could lose even one, then we have no reason to believe that Heaven would have anyone. But that's just me…well, me and the words of Jesus Himself. But take that however you wish since this isn't a theology book. Maybe one day I'll write that one…but as of right now I'll just leave that there.

This is what my friend who I quoted at the start of the chapter was wrestling with. As we spoke I told him that as far as I was convinced, God sovereignty placed him where he was. I went on to tell him that I believed that God had orchestrated all of my pain, my suffering, and the dark night that has haunted me. I also believed that God had done the same for him as well. For him this didn't seem helpful at the time. And maybe it doesn't seem helpful to you. But let me play it out a little bit.

If we are where we are because God has simply allowed for things to happen, if He has placed our suffering, or our good

---

[13] John 6:37-40

in our hands and in the hands of the sinful people that surround us (because we are all sinful people, so everyone is only surrounded by sinful people) then He is simply watching and hoping that the best works out for us. But that's not the God I see in Scripture. I see a God who is never reactive. I see a God who has a plan, and accomplishes it. Every time. Always. So if we follow this logically, if God is not sovereign in bringing us into our suffering, we have no true hope that He can bring us out of it. And if we have no hope that He can bring us out of it, then we don't have a lot of hope that He can use it for our good or His glory. And if that's the case, then we don't have any hope. None. Zero.

But that's not what I have come to find. I have seen that even in the darkest places God is still working around me. And more comforting, He is still working through me. Though I may not always see it, or even want to see it. And even when I try to tell Him that I'm not worth being used anymore.

Sometimes it happens in ways that are annoying in the moment. Places where I have decided that all I want to do is run the other way. Away from God. And in those places He holds me close. I'm not at all saying that He never lets me wander; I wish that were the case. He often does. And each time that happens I find myself to be, once again, a wounded fool. But even in those moments He shows me that no matter how foolish I become, He still is there, He still loves me, He is still for me.

And yet even this has served to make me more and more homesick. Each time I stumble, each time I fall, each time I sin. Each time I am welcomed back and covered with the love of my Abba. Not once I get to the place where I am sorry enough. I need no penance to make Him love me; to even believe so is to doubt the power of what Christ accomplished for us on the cross.

Each time I come back to God after falling and failing I am reminded of the pain and filth of sin, of my sin. And even here, it is never enough to keep God from me. If it were the cross would have no power at all. And because of this, each time I fall I see anew how much I hate being separated from God. How much I wish that I could just be with Him. Always. Forever.

It is in moments like these that I can feel my holy homesickness grow. I long for that city where God will dwell with us. That city which needs no streetlights because God's glory will be so bright that everything is illuminated. Almost as if St John[14] was right when he wrote that where Jesus is, no darkness can stand to stay.

And when I am doing well, I can trust that this place will be my home. I will come to it when I need to. But as someone who knows how a rifle feels; both on my shoulder, and in my mouth, I understand that even this most beautiful promise can become twisted. For if this is the end goal, if everything leads to this end, why not just go? Why should we wait around for another week, month, or year of what seems like hell? Why do we need to see who will be the next person to betray us? Why do we need to keep going to sleep alone, and that's assuming that sleep comes at all? Why wait around for yet another day when the only calls are telemarketers and the only texts come from a record club that I seldom buy anything from?

I am the type of person who tries to follow things logically. That's why I have five points and not just four[15]. And logically there seems to be this idea that if Home is the goal,

---

[14] John 1

[15] If you don't get this reference I would advise looking up and listening to John Piper's series 'TULIP'. It's quite good and I believe that the end result will be that you love Jesus more; at least that is what happened for me.

then I should get there as soon as possible. But at the end of the day there are more things to consider. Someone much smarter than me put it this way, "Therefore, earthy life, when compared with heavenly life, must certainly and readily be condemned and despised. It should never be hated, except to the extent that it makes us liable to sin—through properly speaking our hatred should be toward sin, not life itself. Although we may be so moved with weariness and hatred of this life that we despise its end, we must be prepared to remain in it according to the Lord's will. And so, our weariness won't result in complaining and impatience. For the Lord has stationed us in an outpost, and we must keep guard here until He calls us home. In truth, Paul, being held captive so long in the bonds of the flesh, lamented his condition, and sighed with a burning desire for deliverance. 'Wretched man that I am! Who will deliver me from this body of death?[16]' Nevertheless, that he might submit himself to God's rule, he declared himself ready for whatever might come[17]. He realized his duty to God was to glorify His name, whether by death of life[18]. But it's God's right to decide what best serves His own glory.[19]"

Even now, I often feel this tug. This desire to be Home. This desire to not have to wrestle with a loneliness that is more often pain than not. To not be haunted by sins that still hurt. To no longer have to weigh out if the joy of hope is worth the pain of things hoped for not happening. I feel this desire, but I also know that through it all, I don't have to wait till I get Home to get Jesus. And at the end of the day isn't that the

---

[16]Romans 7:24
[17] Philippians1:23-24
[18] Romans 14:8
[19] Calvin, John. "Meditation on Our Future Life." Edited by Aaron C. Denlinger and Burk Parsons. In *A Little Book on the Christian Life*, 99-100. Orlando, FL: Reformation Trust Publishing, A Division of Ligonier Ministries, 2017. *The Institutes of Christian Religion*.

end goal? Isn't the desire to be Home simply the desire to be with Jesus?

If so, then maybe we all need to remember, myself included, that we were promised trouble. It has always been part of the offer we accepted. Maybe your pastor didn't tell you, but it's always been there. Time and again Jesus makes it clear that we'll have trouble in this world. We'll have pain. We'll have all that He had. But tied to the promise Jesus gave us that said we'd be troubled was the promise that He'd be with us in it[20].

So as much as we long for the time when we shall be able to have Jesus with us all the time, and for all time, we must also remember what we were told. Christ has promised that He would be with us always[21]. That He would never leave nor forsake us[22]. It can often times be hard to believe these promises to be true. But we must remember, as we have looked at already, that at times we must recognize what is true and speak that to ourselves. We must press on past the emotions of the moment and understand that the words spoken by God hold more weight that the ones spoken by us, and the ones spoken by our enemy.

---

[20] John 16:33
[21] Matthew 28:20
[22] Hebrews 13:5

PRAYER:

Abba,
I long for the day when I'll finally be Home.
That place where I no longer need to pray, fast, or weep.
That place where I am no longer tempted and cannot sin.
I long for the day when I no longer need Communion,
For instead I'll have the marriage feast.
Lord, let me arrive to that place where nothing can be defiled.
A place devoid of grief, sorrow, sin, and shame.
A place where there is no separation from You.
A place where I'll never again feel the effects of sin.
The sins of others or the sin of my own making.
Let me long for that place where I shall be complete.
I want to see with perfect sight.
I want to behold Your beauty.
I want to hear and join the chorus of angels.
I want to be where my joy shall be forever complete.
I want to be filled with the truth of who You are.
Here on earth I feel as though I am an ant.
Surrounded by other ants, small and busy.
And just as an ant could never understand me,
I know that I am lacking in my understanding of You.
But when I arrive Home, I shall know You.
I will be with You.
I will be with my true family.
I will stand before You and worship.
I will be there as an heir with Christ.
I will be an eternal member of His body.
I will forever one with Christ, who is forever one with You.
Abba, I look forward to the day when I can worship You Fully.

With every part of me free from the chains of sin and Brokenness.
Teach me to worship You now.
Teach me to read Your word, to pray, to be with other, to love,
All as if I were with You know.
For that is how I am even now seen, in Christ, here[23].

[23] Adapted from 'Heaven Desired' in The Valley of Vision Prayer Book

VII
Shame

"Fear not, for you will not be ashamed; be not confounded, for you will not be disgraced; for you will forget the shame of your youth, and the reproach of your widowhood you will remember no more. For your Maker is your husband, the LORD of hosts is his name; and the Holy One of Israel is your Redeemer, the God of the whole earth he is called."
–Isaiah 54:4-5

"Our hearts all too readily echo the voice of Satan."
–Charles Spurgeon

A few weeks back I made the decision to transfer to Alabama State University. After high school I took a year off to travel, and that turned to almost 10 years off. When I moved back to Alabama, and then when what I moved back for fell out of the picture, I figured that maybe it was time to finally go to college.

While trying to figure out what to do I was able to talk to a few church planters, some that planted churches that are still going, and some that planted churches that are no longer here. And with their advice, along with the advice of a old heads I often run stuff by, I decided to go ahead and get a degree. My goal has long been to plant a church in an urban area and a lot of people I talked to told me that having a way to make tents, to use church vocabulary[1], would be a smart move. So now I'm currently working on a degree that will allow me to teach high school English as a way to make money while I, Lord willing, plant a church in an urban center a few years from now.

---

[1] The Apostle Paul made tents as a way of funding his missionary trips (Acts 18:2-3). So 'tent making' is Christian slang for having a job while also being in ministry. This is also commonly referred to as being bi-vocational

But right now I live in Opelika, Alabama, and Alabama State is in Montgomery. If you're not familiar with the state of Alabama, that means I have a sixty mile commute to make it down to the campus.

A few years back, while I was working for my dad's ministry, Harvest Evangelism[2], and planning mission trips I had a trip to Ireland planned. The plan for this trip was to attend a conference and then scout out a possible future trip to the island that I had once called home. The plan was for another guy who worked with me at the time and I to spend about two weeks there. I was exited to be back. And so we had plans to fly from Atlanta, GA to Shannon, Ireland and then head down to Cork City (the real capitol of Ireland). But on the way to Atlanta we had to drive up through a mean storm. The type of storm that makes a lot of people stop at a truck stop and eat food they don't really want. But we had a to be at the airport at a certain time, so we drove on.

About 30 miles south of the airport we ended up hitting a patch of water and the truck we were in hydroplaned. We hit the guardrail and we rolled the truck six times that I counted; stopping a truck going 70 miles an hour isn't an easy feat.

When we stopped rolling I was the only one conscious. A few years before I had trained and fought MMA, although as I have said earlier I had a short career. And when training, one of the biggest things that I was taught was to control adrenaline. When fighting you have to see things coming. You have to be able to see each problem and solve them as they come (or make sure you keep the guy close to your corner and listen to your loud coach). You have to be able to channel your adrenaline and use it as a tool in your tool belt. So when we wrecked the truck I saw that there were a

---

[2]www.harvestevangelism.org

number of things that were problems and each needed to be solved in order. I called out to the guys in the truck. Two of the three answered. Then we had to see if anyone could get out. No one could. I had to elbow out what remained of the back window, and then begin to pull out the other guys. I pulled out two of them and let the third remain, because I honestly thought that he was dead in the moment. He wasn't. But he had broken his neck and his back in a number of places. Had I tried to pull him out I most likely would have killed one of my dear friends in an attempt to save him.

Though that story could go on further, the largest part is that all of us survived. And my mate who broke his back and his neck is now doing well and working for a ministry in Philly. But even though everyone that was in that truck made it out, that wreck scared me in a lot of ways. More than I even realized at the time it happened.

Last week when I was driving back from class in Montgomery I ended up having to drive through another crazy storm. It seemed as if the lightning lit the sky as bright as noonday every few moments. Driving home I turned into that annoying person going 45 on the interstate. Because even though that wreck was years in the past, I couldn't help but remember it because of what I was going through. Each time the rain picked up, and each time the car slid even an inch all I could think of was a truck that rolled a few years back. All I could think was of that wreck. And though I hate to admit it, driving in the rain scares me to this day.

About two week ago I gave flowers to a girl for the first time in a long time. The last time I had done this, the girl I gave flowers to had promised to share my name. I had a crush on this girl for a while, and I found out that her favorite flowers were hydrangeas. So I found one that was in bloom and got it. I took it home and planted it in one of the pots that I happened to have laying around my front porch. That night I took it over to her place and gave it to her. And she is the type of girl that any guy would be lucky to buy flowers for. If you met her, you'd probably want to buy her flowers too.

Maybe it doesn't seem like a big thing. But I once read that giving a girl flowers can change the world[3]. And if you take the time to read why, you might just begin to agree with the both of us that these are the types of things that can.

I showed up around 7-o-clock and we sat and talked till almost midnight. After that I drove back home feeling like I was on to of the moon. On the way home I texted her 'sweet dreams', and to be able to tell that to a pretty girl again just added to happiness I was feeling in the moment. I have been accused of being a hopeless romantic more than once, and that night I was happy to be able to have someone to feel hopelessly romantic for. That was a Monday night. But Tuesday came with no word from her. And after Tuesday came the rest of the week.

Maybe I made more of things than I should have, knowing myself this was exactly what happened, but as the week progressed I began to hear the echo of voices that I had long learned to ignore. As I have mentioned earlier in this book, my engagement ended over the phone. But after we had ended everything I kept tying to make things work. Finally I got to the place where I said I would call my ex-fiancé one last time. If she answered, I would take it as a sign that God would put us back together. If she didn't pick up, then I would try and forget both her and her number. I called. She picked up. I drove up that next weekend and we spent a few days at her aunt's place at the Chesapeake Bay. For about two months we were back together. We talked about another

---

[3] https://seandietrich.com/girls/

date to get married. She even quit her job and we found a place for her to live here in Alabama so she could live here before we got married.

We talked about how much it hurt me that she ended things over the phone, and she said that even if it didn't work out this time that it couldn't end over a phone call. And that time around she was honest. Because the second time around it ended with a text that said she was sorry for hurting me, but that she couldn't go through with our plans.

After giving hydrangeas to this girl two weeks back, I felt like after a long season of pulling the short straw in this area and praying only to have my echo be the answer, there might just be a change in the wind. Then, after not hearing from her for a week, so much came flooding back. After getting that text from a girl I was planning to marry, I felt for so long that I wasn't worth anything more than a text. And a text doesn't mean anything. Which is another reason I hate being single now. Texting sucks. What happened to long calls after 9pm when you had free minutes? But then again what happened to opening doors, standing when you met a pretty girl, and offering to light up someone's smoke without trying to take them home because you did.

Though this girl with a newly potted hydrangea never gave me any reason to feel shame. I thought that a date would be fun, she didn't. And that's nothing to get upset about. But her reaction made all the shame that I had battled for so long come flooding back in. I had placed my past in a box and shoved it away. But being told no to a date made all the shame I had carefully packed away spill out in front of me once again.

I'm not sure how much shame you have wrestled with. And I say how much, because I know we all wrestle with shame. But for me, I began to feel all the voices of my past speak to my inadequacy. Speaking to all the ways that I was not good enough, all the places where I had failed, all the places where I should have been better. I was told that if only I was good enough, if only I was better, if only I hadn't messed up in this area or that. If only…then I would be ok. Then I wouldn't be battling this brokenness, loneliness, and shame.

And shame has a funny way of taking you back to each and every thing that you have ever done wrong, every sin that you still wrestle with. The sins that hurt you, and even more so—those that hurt other. I have a few of the latter that I still wish I could ask forgiveness for. But a lot of us have sinned against people who we can't just go back and ask forgiveness from. And an 'ex' can be at the top of that list. And feeling as though you might not be forgiven is like throwing gas on the fire of shame in our hearts.

I have shared a lot of ways how my brokenness started with a girl who sinned with me and then sinned against me. But what I haven't spoken to much until now is that when I was sinned against I didn't act like Jesus. Because I knew her, I aimed at the places that I knew were the most tender. In the first chapter I shared a quote from Tim Keller about how we often respond in sinful anger when we feel threatened. And I sinned against this broken and beautiful girl. I threatened to share things that would have shamed her. And though I never would have, I just wished that we would fight again instead of keeping silent, she will never know that. And because I knew her I knew how to say things that would wound her soul. And I said them as forceful as I could. I knew the places in her heart that would wound her the most. And I took careful aim at each and every one of them. And the shame of that came back over me.

So often we can find ourselves, or at least I can find myself, in a place where we look back over our story and see all our faults and failures and allow those to be the things that define us. And we live in a culture where that is surely the case. In one of my education classes at Alabama State, my professor tells us on an almost weekly basis that we must know what is going on in our communities. Because, she tells us, that though we can have the right answer a thousand times, that single time we are found to not know, our students will see us as someone who knows nothing at all. Even if we had the answer every time before.

But what can we do then? For I am sure that you, like me, have more scars and wounds on your soul than you would like to admit. Scars and wounds caused by others, and often more shameful, scars and wounds caused by ourselves.

I have often loved to read Brennan Manning. For me he has become the greatest avenue that the Holy Spirit has used to show me the true, fatherly, graceful love of God. It is through his writing that I have truly come to see God the Father as my Abba. For I can easily explain the doctrine of adoption in a way that would be theologically correct, but a lot of the time I often feel as though I could be a better soldier than a son. And often I wish that God thought the same way. Somehow it seems easier, simpler. In his book, *The Furious Longing of God,* Manning begins his introduction in a way that has spoken life to me on this issue:

"I'm Brennan. I'm an alcoholic.
How I got there, why I left, why I went back, is the story of my life.
But it is not the whole story.

I'm Brennan. I'm a Catholic.
How I got there, why I left there, why I went back, is also the story of my life.
But it is not the whole story.

I'm Brennan. I was a priest, but I am no longer a priest. I was a married man but am no longer a married man.
How I got to those places, why I left those places, is the story of my life too.
But it is not the whole story.

I'm Brennan. I'm a sinner, saved by grace.
That is the larger and more important story.
Only God, in His fury, knows the whole of it.[4]"

If you are anything like me, then in reading that you felt an immediate pushback. For amongst the things listed there are things that would make me want to back away. I can see things that I disagree with. But deeper than all of that I can see an honesty that I wish that I could have. I can see someone who has truly understood that the only opinion that matters is that of our God. Our Abba, as Brennan puts it. Someone who understands that once we know what God thinks of us, we are free to be honest with those around us, and even harder, with ourselves.

And maybe that is part of what this book has become for me, a place where I can echo Brennan. Echoing his honesty; honesty about the dark places in my own story and trust that the light of Christ will always drive out darkness. Even when we find that darkness is in us instead of 'out there' where we were told in Sunday School it would always come from.

In the first chapter I shared two songs that I have often gone back to time and again in this season of darkness and light. I hope that you were able to listen to them, and I hope that they were able to speak to you half as much as they spoke to me. But there is another song which I have also bellowed out as if

---

[4] "Intro." *The Furious Longing of God*, by Brennan Manning, David C. Cook, 2009, pp. 17–18.

the words were taken from my own soul[5]. Within the song are the lyrics, "There's something mumbling in my mind. Secrets that you weren't meant to find. You thought you knew me so well, and I will see you in Hell before I let you live to tell what you've seen. There's something dark inside of me."

I know that many of you reading that will wonder why I would choose to include such a quote. I mean, I am saying that I would rather see someone in Hell than to be found out. But I'm sure that when we all begin to be honest many of us feel the same way. What if everything that we ever said, did, or thought was suddenly on the front page of your local newspaper. Would you stick around to see what the result would be, or would you buy a one-way ticket to anywhere? What if everything that caused us such shame was brought to the forefront of the world? What if it was suddenly no longer trapped away in the dark places of our past but out in the light for all to see? For even Jesus says that what's done in the darkness will be brought out eventually[6]. And I have to wonder if such a promise should cause me to celebration or fear?

For the longest time I hated the idea of people finding out the things that I have tried to keep hidden away in the recesses of my past. Placed away in the dungeon of my soul. I thought that I had killed these things. But much to my dismay, and fear, they had turned to the ghosts that would haunt me.

This morning I found myself reading through John 4. That is the chapter that tells of Jesus and the Samaritan woman, or the woman at the well as she has come to be known. Maybe you're familiar with the story, maybe not. But in this chapter

---

[5] There's Something Dark by Dustin Kensrue
[6] Luke 8:17

John records that Jesus sits down because He was worn out, which is the first thing I think most people overlook. Jesus, the Word of God, King of Kings, the One who has always been, He who had the strength to make the cosmos at the command of our Father, made himself to be wrapped in humanity and because of this became so worn out that He had to stop and rest for a spell.

While sitting there a woman came in the middle of the day to draw up water from the well He was sitting by, the Well of Jacob. And maybe this means nothing to you. But in this day-and-age people didn't really do that. It would have been hot and arid at this time of day. So people would go to the well together in the cool of the morning, or in the last light of evening. It was less physically taxing since it wasn't as hot at these times, and on top of that it was a social thing. It was where they came together as a community and did life together. But here was a woman coming in the heat of the day, and coming alone. To the original readers this would have sent up a red flag with the question, "Why was she there then? Why was she there alone?" So keep those questions in your mind as the story progresses.

As they sat there Jesus asked this woman for water. They speak and Jesus ends up telling her that He could give her living water. The type we talked about in chapter four. He was offering water that would never run out, water that would mean she'd never have to come back to this well alone and in the heat of the day.

Then Jesus does what He does often, He goes right to her heart. He point to the fact that she'd had five past husbands and was now in a place where she way swapping sex for rent. Or to say it in a more culturally sensitive way for the Western world, she was cohabitating with someone.

So here was the answer to the question that we should have asked at the start of the story. Why go to the well alone? Why go when she knew no one else would be there? And the answerer is the same one that causes you and I to isolate to this day. Shame.

Place yourself in the story. Imagine being her and getting water with the rest of the women from the town. How many times had she gone before the questioning looks of the other women started to wound? How many times did she walk up to a conversation only to have it stop, with her knowing full well she was the topic of conversation before? How long did it take for the pain of going alone in the mid-day sun to become easier than the pain of her own shame being on full display in the cooler hours? How long had she held out for? Maybe she lasted as long as it took for the pain of isolation to become easier than the pain of her shame. For in this story we are often told to be like Jesus, taking time to talk to those who are full of shame. But if we are honest we are the woman. We are the ones full of shame. We are the ones in need of an encounter with Jesus. We are the ones who need this living water. We are the ones who find ourselves alone because we fear being found out, or maybe because we already have been.

Jesus goes right for the kill. He doesn't do what most people in the church do. He goes right to the heart of the matter. He didn't try to turn a blind eye, He didn't make light of her sin, He didn't avoid the topic. But knowing all of her story, He tells her that this living water offer is still there. And what does she do? For Jesus wasn't the first one to point to the places in her life that caused the shame she now carried. But Jesus was the first one to allow her to echo the words that Brennan wrote, " How I got to those places, why I left those places, is the story of my life. But it is not the whole story."

There is something that happens when someone allows us to own what we have done, who we have been, and see it in another light. This woman ended up running back into town, back to the people she went to the well at midday to avoid, and she told them to "Come see the man who has told me all that I had done[7]." Somehow this simple encounter with Jesus changed everything. Because people knowing everything she had ever done was the reason she was alone at the well to begin with.

We live in a culture, more in the Church than elsewhere unfortunately, that so often stands ready to crucify us for any failing or failure we commit. And worse than our culture, we are ready to do this to ourselves, or we hide ourselves from the world so that those around us won't have a chance to nail us up and leave us out to hang.

So again we must ask, what made the difference? When those around this woman knew all that she had done, the heavy chains of shame weighed her down. But when Christ spoke into these same areas her chains seemed to suddenly fall off. Why?

I believe that the answer lies in light of who Jesus is, and what He sees when He looks upon those who will be His own. This woman hid herself because those who heard her story used it to define her. To them she was nothing more that what she had done. But when Jesus pointed out all of the same things He was not doing so in a way that added to the burden she carried, but to take it from her altogether.

Maybe Jesus was the first person in her entire life that saw her story so far, and yet knew that wasn't going to be how it ended. Jesus saw her. He saw past her past, past her sin, past

---

[7] John 4:29

her shame, past her wounds, and He saw her. He saw her as someone defined by who He made her to be, not what she had made of herself.

As St. Paul writes, "For our sake He (the Father) made Him (Christ) to be sin who knew no sin, so that in Him we might become the righteousness of God.[8]" I once heard that in response to this verse Martin Luther added that on the cross Christ did not take the sin of the drunkard and the prostitute, but became them.

And that is why this woman, and how we, can allow Jesus to see all of our shame and respond with joy. We can see these things as what will kill us. And that is true. But Jesus became known for telling dead people they weren't allowed to hang out in graves anymore. Or as someone else who was caught in a moment of shame and then met Jesus put it, "Slowly I came back to life. I'd been one of the people Ezekiel comes upon in the valley of dry bones—people who had really given up, who were lifeless and without hope. But because of Ezekiel's presence, breath comes upon them; Spirit and kindness revive them.[9]"

Or to quote another, "The cross destroys the false notion of our own strength that we've dared to entertain, and it destroys that hypocrisy in which we have taken refuge and pleasure. It strips us of carnal self-confidence, and thus humbling us, instructs us to cast ourselves on God alone so that we won't be crushed or defeated. Such victory is followed by hope, since the Lord—by providing what He has promised—establishes His truthfulness for what lies ahead. Even for these reasons alone, it's clear how vital the

---

[8] 2 Corinthians 5:21

[9] Lamott, Anne. "Overture: Lily Pads." *Traveling Mercies: Some Thoughts on Faith*, Anchor Books, 2006, p. 44

discipline of the cross is for us. It's no little thing to be stripped of our blind self-love and thus to be made aware of our own weakness. Moreover, having been impressed with our own weakness, we learn to despair of ourselves. Then, having despaired of ourselves, we transfer our trust to God. Next, we rest in our trust in God, and we rely on His help and preserve unconquered to the end. Then standing on His grace, we see that He is true to His promises. Finally, being confident in the certainty of His promises, our hope is strengthened.[10]"

So here we find the answer to the question of our shame. And the answer is the cross. For it is only here that we can take all of the things which have scared us and see them taken away. It is only because Jesus allowed Himself to be scarred that we need not fear the ones which we bear. It is only when we walk to the foot of the cross that we can admit to all of our failures and yet walk away with a victory that we could never earn.

The cross stands to tell us that as bad as we see the things that cause our shame, and they are actually much worse than that, the cross is so much better than we could have ever dared imagine. For though we have done much that is shameful, Jesus took that shame from us and killed it on His cross[11]. And if you are someone who belongs to Christ, then all of your past belongs to Him as well. So to try and take your past sins and use them as a validation to hold onto shame is to steal that which now belongs to Jesus and try to offer it back to Him.

---

[10] Calvin, John. "Bearing Our Cross Is A Part Of Self-Denial." *A Little Book on the Christian Life*, edited by Burk Parsons. translated by Aaron C. Denlinger, Reformation Trust Publishing, A Division of Ligonier Ministries, 2017, pp. 63–64.

[11] Hebrews 12:2

So even though our past may often come back to haunt us (and it will from time to time), we must remember that when we trust our past over our savior, it is not ourselves who we are trusting. But as our first parents in the garden, we are trusting a snake more than a Savior. For our shame is linked to our sins. Our shame stands only to condemn us, but "There is therefore now no condemnation for those who are in Christ Jesus. For the law of the Spirit of life has set you free in Christ Jesus from the law of sin and death. For God has done what the law, weakened by the flesh, could not do. By sending his own Son in the likeness of sinful flesh and for sin, he condemned sin in the flesh, in order that the righteous requirement of the law might be fulfilled in us, who walk not according to the flesh but according to the Spirit. For those who live according to the flesh set their minds on the things of the flesh, but those who live according to the Spirit set their minds on the things of the Spirit. For to set the mind on the flesh is death, but to set the mind on the Spirit is life and peace. For the mind that is set on the flesh is hostile to God, for it does not submit to God's law; indeed, it cannot. Those who are in the flesh cannot please God. You, however, are not in the flesh but in the Spirit, if in fact the Spirit of God dwells in you. Anyone who does not have the Spirit of Christ does not belong to him. But if Christ is in you, although the body is dead because of sin, the Spirit is life because of righteousness. If the Spirit of him who raised Jesus from the dead dwells in you, he who raised Christ Jesus from the dead will also give life to your mortal bodies through his Spirit who dwells in you.[12]"

---

[12] Romans 8:1-11

PRAYER:

Abba,
Next to you I am nothing. I am fleeting, here for a moment
Then gone.
Because of my sins I have forfeited Your favor,
I have been become deformed,
I should be forever banished.
Your law shows me that my sins curse me.
As much as I try I could never deliver myself from this fate.
And because of this I find myself in complete despair.
But where I could do nothing, You have done everything.
Without my actions, or even my desires,
You made a plan from before time to rescue me.
This plan was in line with who You are, a Perfect Father.
And this plan was so amazing that angels are astounded by
Your love.
And Jesus, who is the Word, proclaims this in all glory and
Goodness.
He draws close to me, invites me, calls me.
Let me, knowing my sins and shame,
Find Jesus, alone, as the power of my salvation.
Let me see His death as the only thing that brings me relief.
Let me see Jesus as my greatest blessing.
Help me always be focused on the cross.
Let me understand that because of the cross,
What anyone, including myself, says is false.
And only that which You speak over me is true.
Let the cross teach me to be humble.
Let the cross teach me to be die to myself.
Let me be filled with grace to love others, and myself.
Let me have the faith to trust that You love me, always.
Let me have the hope I need to lift up my head.

Let Your love fill me and bind my heart only to Jesus,
The one who died and rose for me.
Because of this let me be more thankful for your mercy,
More humble when you correct me,
More passionate to serve You,
More on guard against the sin and lies that lives in me,
More content where You have me,
And more useful to You and to others[13].

---

[13] Adapted from 'Deliverance' in The Valley Of Vision Prayer Book

VIII
Identity

"See what kind of love the Father has given to us, that we should be called children of God; and so we are. The reason why the world does not know us is that is did not know Him. Beloved, we are God's children now, and what we will be has not yet appeared; but we know that when He appears we shall be like Him, because we shall see Him as He is."
-1 John 3:1-2

"Define yourself radically as one beloved by God. This is the true self. Every other identity is an illusion."
–Brennan Manning

Figuring out who we are is one of the hardest things that we can do in life. It's why we were all a bit crazy in High School. The questions of 'Who am I?' and 'What should I do with my life?' can easily become the focus of so much of our mental capacity. This question can make us question everything that we have previously known or believed.

But we graduate High School, move on into adulthood and start to form our own identity. Some of us stick around our hometown and allow our identity to be shaped by the places we grew up. Some of us move off and define ourselves as those who 'got away'. But I have found that most people allow others to speak who they are or 'should be' and what they should be doing and allow that to become how they define themselves. For most of us, the years following High School into our early 20's will shape who we'll be the rest of our lives. Most people aren't given the severe mercy of a mulligan.

But in the end, we all form an identify for ourselves. Because who we are and how we define ourselves is truly important. It shapes what we do and why we do it. It becomes the lens through which we view the world and the things that take place in it. It's why people act the way they do and, more than that, it's why people react the ways that they do. We can often arrive at the place where our identity is so wrapped up in the things that give us our identity that we couldn't imagine a life without them, and don't know how to live if, and when, they are taken away from us. In all honesty, our god is the thing that we could not imagine life without. No matter where we choose to spend our Sundays.

In the summer of 2016 all the things that I couldn't imagine life without, all my gods, were suddenly taken away from me. And I didn't know what to do. I didn't know who I was without them.

My entire adult life I was marked by what I was doing, it was who I was. I even forfeited the close friendship that people form in their 'college years'. Most people I knew asked each other how they were doing, and they just asked me where I was going. Christ had brought me back to Himself when I was 18-19 years old and pretty much from that time on my life was defined by what I was doing, and where I was going. As I said in the first chapter, I knew I was only a tool that God was using. But again, I felt as if I must have been a damn good one. And I liked it that way. To be honest, there are still days I wish I could go back to it. I think that eventually I will, but this time around I'll be able to see it in a different light.

One of the questions I like to ask people is what comes to mind when they think of God. He has shown Himself to us in a myriad of ways through the Scriptures, but people often have one of those ways in the forefront of their mind when thinking of God.

For some people it's Savior. And what a beautiful way to think about God. For He was the one who saved us from our sin and the shame that follows. And often, but not always, people who think of God as Savior first have a past that shows boldly the ability of God to save us from our sins as well as the sins of others.

Other people will respond that what comes to mind when the question of God is asked is that of a Friend who sticks closer than a brother. Which is yet another beautiful showcase of the love of Christ. For He is the One who has promised to never leave us or forsake us. And often people who see God this way have been forced to experience Him in such a way because they don't have many others to use that term for. Through lack of true and deep connection with others the closeness of Christ through the Holy Spirit becomes a source of life.

And others may yet respond to this question with the understanding of God as provider. And, oh, how He can provide. When we read the history of our family, the people of God, we see time and again how God shows up and provides just what was needed; just when it was needed it[1]. And if we are honest, any of us who have walked with Jesus for any time can point to times that He showed up right when He needed to, and with just what we needed. Often people who see God this way have many stories of God doing just that. And often doing it in a way that would bring you to tears at the love and provision of Abba for His children.

For me, when I thought of God, I thought of the King. I permeated every good action I made, every prayer I prayed, and every plan I made and asked God to sign off on.

I grew up wrestling, and I was never one of the best wrestlers. Maybe, if I hadn't started finding little white lines to speed me up I could have been. But I also wasn't one of

---

[1] I think there is no better place to see this than a biography of George Müller

the worst. I have a few gold medals, but not as many as my older brother.

While I was wrestling I would always try to position myself around better wrestlers. By doing this I was forcing myself to be better. As a guy, when I saw tough dudes, I wanted to be tougher. When I saw guys who were working their tails off, I wanted to follow suit. And in some ways, this is how I saw Jesus after He brought me back to Himself. Because one of the reasons I didn't like Jesus in high school was because it seemed like I could kick His ass.

The picture that we have of Jesus in Scripture, Jesus as He is now, is one of power. He's the commander of Heaven's armies[2], He's the sovereign ruler of all creation[3], it's He who'll judge the living and the dead[4], and when He comes back to fight the collected armies of the Devil and the Anti-Christ it's He alone who fights[5]. The rest of His army just follows Him like a group of fan-girls. There is finally an army that thinks it can take Him. And He pulls a sword from His mouth and kills everyone who dared to think they could last a single round with the King of Heaven.

When I though of God, this is who I saw. And everything else went through this lens. Though I didn't know it at the time, only allowing myself to intimately see God in this way prevented me from truly experiencing Him in any other. I had isolated this aspect of who God is and made it larger than anything else. And in so doing I created a characture of God that I could worship instead of seeing Him as He truly is. He is the powerful King of all, but He's also more. Much, much more.

---

[2] Revelation 19:11-16
[3] Colossians 1:15-20
[4] Matthew 25:31-32
[5] Revelation 19

And so I positioned myself as close to Him as I could. At least that is what I was thinking at the time. I chased after everything I thought was Jesus telling me to follow. Looking back I don't think that doing so was sinful, but I don't think it was all for the most God glorifying reasons. In my own little way I was trying to be Indiana Jones with a Bible. Taking a trip on two weeks notice and not seeing a white dude outside of the mirror for weeks on end. And when I got home I was a 22-year-old church planter. That was who I was, or at least who I wanted to be. That was my identity. Who I was became what I did for Jesus, and somewhere along the way I had lost Jesus while trying to follow Him.

Then at 24 I had allowed my identity to become shaped by the girl I was planning to marry. And though I didn't know it until both of these things were no longer in my life, together they shaped my entire identity.

Wherever I went I really only had two things to talk about. And I could get there in 10,000 ways, but in the end all my conversations got to one of two places. What I was doing, or planning on doing for God. And the person I thought would be there with me for the journey. The first of these was the mission that God had given me, and the second was a person that I believed God had placed in my life. And because God had, seemingly, given me both of these things, I believed that they were allowed to shape me as only God should, or truly can.

Though I couldn't see it at the time. I had allowed the things which God had given me to take the place of God in my life; and because of that, I began to worship those things.

A number of years ago I spent a few months in India. While I was there it was easy to see what people worshiped. It seemed as if each person had a god the size of a G.I. Joe placed in a prominent place, as if to watch over them. I was also able to visit a few temples and see these same gods of theirs, only much larger, carved into stone and cast in gold. What they worshiped was quite evident.

In the western world it's a bit harder to see what people worship. And it was hard for me to see what I was worshiping. Though I would speak of worshiping the true God of the Bible, in reality I wasn't. I was worshiping something else and slapping a fish sticker on the back of it all, thinking that would make it right.

Through times of ministry I had come to the place where I believed, though I couldn't fully see it at the time, what I was doing was all for God. My identity was wrapped up in what I was doing and less in who I was doing it for. I was more pleased with myself when I got an 'atta-boy' after a sermon than I was when I read of Christ's acceptance of me. I felt more loved when a girl with curly hair said that she loved me then when Abba said the same thing.

I had taken my gifts and I turned them into my gods. Who I was had become shaped by these things, and as a result I started to become shaped less by Christ and more by what I thought I should be, where I thought I should be, what I thought I should be doing, and who would be doing it with me.

I don't know if you've ever been in a place where what defines you is no longer there. But it hurts, and more than the pain, there is also a fear that coincides with it. The question of 'Who am I?' that should have been answered years ago comes back with a vengeance. But this time everyone else seems to have it figured out. Which makes wrestling with it all over again all the harder.

One of the things that surprised me was that I got to the place in my brokenness that I became defined by it. Each time I had a conversation I found some way to speak of how I had been hurt, some way to put my pain on display. As if this was who I had become. And it a way, it was.

I was longing to be fixed, but through it all I got to the place where I wasn't sure if I ever would be. I never said it, at least not to anyone else. But it was there. A feeling that I had become one who was broken, and I wasn't sure if I would ever get back to the place where I was whole. And in a strange way, I wasn't sure if I ever wanted to be since at least I understood my brokenness. And it seemed in those times that an identity rooted in my brokenness was less frightful than another season of not knowing what my identity was.

For a number of months, while our schedules lined up, my pastor at that Presbyterian church and I would meet up for sermon prep. It was always a great time. He would open his notes and we would go through what he was going to preach. On occasion we would go back and forth on stuff, him being Presbyterian and me being a bad Baptist, it came around to who to dunk and how more than once. I can remember one time we were sitting in his office sipping whiskey and going over something, 2 John if I remember correctly. But as we spoke the conversation changed from what he was going to preach in the future to what we were each wrestling with in the present. We took the time to actually know each other and that means times of being vulnerable. Something which can often be much harder done than said.

"You have to stop believing the lie that you need to get ready for when your life starts back…"

I'm not even sure I can remember exactly what was said that lead to this comment. But he had pointed at something that had haunting me. Deep down I believed that Jesus had not only taken my identity, but He had taken my life. And I was just waiting around for Him to give it back. When He had taken away what I used to define myself, it broke me. And then at some point I just let that brokenness take the place of what was taken away. Just when and were this happened I couldn't say. But it took a dear friend sitting in his office for me to begin to see it.

I'm not sure if you've ever been in a place where you have been defined by your brokenness, or if you are there now. But it becomes the topic of almost every conversation. You direct things in that path, even without knowing it, and then you show the places that you've been wounded. Reopening them, almost doing it so that they'll keep from scaring over. Fearing that if they heal you'll be left with no identity once again. And that can easily produce a kind of pain that's worse than the pain of being broken. For wounds which stay open become infected.

Over the years I have come to see Ephesians 1 as one of the most beautiful things I have ever seen. And I've seen at least my share beautiful things.

I think that it's because this chapter, or at least the first 14 verses stand 'contra mundum', against the world. It stands at odds with everything that should be true, instead speaking that which can only be true in light of Christ turning our world on its head. Each time I find myself in a place where I am shaped by anything other than the gospel these verses have been a gold standard for me. They tell me who I really am, and they can do the same for you. For these verses speak that which it true of all of us who are found in Christ. Anything that would tell you different is the lie.

If you're not familiar with the verses off the top of your head, here they are:

"Blessed be the God and Father of our Lord Jesus Christ, who has blessed us in Christ with every spiritual blessing in the heavenly places, even as He chose us in Him before the foundation of the world, that we should be holy and blameless before Him. In love He predestined us for adoption to Himself as sons through Jesus Christ, according to the purpose of His will, to the praise of His glorious grace, with which He has blessed us in the Beloved. In Him we have redemption through His blood, the forgiveness of our trespasses, according to the riches of His grace, which He lavished upon us, in all wisdom and insight making known to us the mystery of His will, according to His purpose, which He set forth in Christ as a plan for the fullness of time, to unite all things in Him, things in heaven and things on earth. In Him we have obtained an inheritance, having been predestined according to the purpose of Him who works all things according to the counsel of His will, so that we who were the first to hope in Christ might be to the praise of His glory. In Him you also, when you heard the word of truth, the gospel of your salvation, and believed in Him, were sealed with the promised Holy Spirit, who is the guarantee of our inheritance until we acquire possession of it, to the praise of His glory.[6]"

I hope that you were able to catch all that was said of you in those few sentences. Or if you go back to the original Greek, that entire passage was a single sentence. I once heard a pastor say that Paul was so exited about who we were in Christ that he forgot to punctuate[7]. But within these verses I have been able to come back to the place where I once had fallen in love with Jesus. These verses called me back to who I truly was. It was in these verses years ago in Ireland that I truly began to be shaped into the person I would become, and

---

[6] Ephesians 1:3-14

[7] That statement was given by Mark Driscoll when he preached through Ephesians at Mars Hill Church. At least that's what I remember, I know it was Driscoll and I used to listen to a lot of him. So I can't remember the exact sermon.

it has been in these verses that the Spirit has reshaped me into the person I shall always be.

Earlier in this book I spoke of getting homework from the counselor that I saw for a year or so. And if you have gotten this far I hope that I can give you a little bit as well[8]. Take these verses and speak them over yourself. Because so often our identify is shaped by the things that we say over ourselves. I'm not saying that I think that the prosperity preachers are right when they say that we can just claim something, trust me. I've tried even that in my desperation. And I don't think that we should listen to Oprah when she tells her fans to simply visualize what their future holds. But there is power in the tongue. Even if that power is only to say something until we believe it to be true. To understand this we need look no further than the psalmists who often speak to their own soul.

As for me, I had gotten to the place where I was self sabotaging. I don't think that it was a conscious thing. But I had believed that who I was, was someone who was broken. I wasn't worth the effort. And I could put forth the evidence to show you how I was right. Each time reopening a wound that Jesus was trying to heal. Each time not letting Him do the thing which I was praying He would.

And yet, even in those places Jesus used a friends voice in that old church office and His own words to begin my healing process. Not that it was easy, and not that it was quick. I can't even tell you that this process is completed even now. Deep wounds rarely heal quickly. And to be honest, I find myself weary of people who would tell you any different. And even if they are healed quickly, we're all still left with the scars. But at the end of the day, if Jesus has a

---

[8] I will include it before the prayer at the end of this chapter.

few scars, then maybe it's ok for us to have a few as well. But that's just my opinion.

This semester I enrolled in a public speaking class. I tried to get out of it. I argued with my advisor that I had a few hundred hours of public speaking with a few sermons and pictures online to prove it. But none of that seemed to matter when the school would get paid for three credit hours.

The first speech that the class was given was a speech called 'me in a bag'. The idea of the speech was that we would have to place eight things in a bag and then pull them out, showing who we are.

But what the professor was really asking us was to tell her what our identity was. Being a class half filled with 18-year-old freshman there were some funny answers. Some serious ones. Some sad.

When it was my turn I took out things from the different places I have been. My old house key from when I lived in Ireland (sorry for stealing it Olly), an old business card that had 'Pastor' before my name from when I planted a church. A coin I still have from the few months I spent in India. Then I got down to my 7th thing. I pulled out an old coffee cup. I spent around 5 years in the craft coffee industry[9] and talked about how I had an identity that was shaped in a lot of ways by being behind a bar. I was the guy that everyone called friend but they only saw when they needed a pick-me-up. As I spoke I swirled the cup on my finger…then without warning I smashed it on the ground. It shocked more than a few of my classmates, but I did it because in many ways I am

---

[9] Thanks Wade for giving me a shot to work with you and for all those late nights closing down the shop with 'Wake Up Lattes'. Even if those lattes ended up getting me in trouble. I can't begin to tell you how dearly I still hold those memories.

still broken. I told the class, once they settled down from the scare of something breaking, that who I was was a broken person. And I did it because each thing I had pulled out of that bag before, including the mug, had represented an identity which was used to define me for a season of my life. But each of those identities only shattered in the end, and as a result broke me in the process.

But I had one thing left in that paper bag. When I moved home from Ireland my best friend at the time, Patrick, and another dear friend, Maurice, took me to the airport in Dublin to fly back to Alabama. On the way we stopped for a Guinness and then when we got to the airport for our final goodbyes Patrick gave me his bible. I still read it from time to time. Both the Word printed in it and the words he had written in it. Maybe I do so as a way to cling onto a season I often look back on with rose-colored glasses. But, in my public speaking class, I took it out and threw it on the table at the front of the room. Because the real question of the assignment was the question of identity.

And though I had been shaped by each thing I pulled out before that Bible, and had been broken by each one, what God says to me and what He says about me is the only thing that truly has the power to shape me. It is the only thing that has the authority to give me an identity that will last.

And if you let it, you can do the same thing. Although I learned that you might not want to shatter a coffee mug on the floor the first day of class. Even if you end up with bonus points for the speech.

In this season, in my brokenness, I have found something out. Each of us, if we live long enough, eventually becomes a broken person. Each of us has things that have wounded us and things that have broken us. The only question is if we'll keep opening up the wounds to the point where they become infected. Or if we'll allow Jesus to heal those wounds which seek to define us.

The question is not what we have in our bag. But what is the last thing we'll pull out. For too long I let that broken cup be the last thing. I let my brokenness have the last word. I had allowed myself to believe that since Jesus had stolen what shaped my identity, my life was on hold until He gave me something back. All the while blind to the fact that He already had. I was just too caught up with other things to see it.

I have no clue what your identity is. But if you're anything like me, it's not what it needs to be. Monday morning you might be totally content with where God has you, and you might be fully shaped by what He has said to you. Then by dinnertime you have a list of everything that you need for your life to start. Maybe you waste too much time on social media because who you appear to be online is a little better than who you are in real life. Maybe it's safer to put up who you wish you were, and be able to see all the likes in response. Maybe there aren't any likes to be had, and that is what you use to shape you.

But what I do know is that each of us, this side of Home, is more than a little bit broken. Even with a Bible on the podium there is still a broken cup shattered on the floor. But there comes a point for all of us when we have to find the broom and sweep it up all the broken pieces.

That doesn't mean that you won't still feel it from time to time. And that doesn't mean that it won't hurt. Most likely it'll hurt a lot. But it means that we begin to move past it. I wish I could tell you just what that timeline will be, but Lord knows I'm still finding broken pieces each time I try to clean up.

The only difference now is that they are reminders of where I have been, not where I am now.

Back to those verses in Ephesians. I know that you didn't get everything it said. I have been reading it for years and haven't gotten it all. I could write another book just on those verses and have things missing. I could preach a sermon on every word and at the end I would be found lacking. But within them we are told who we are. Because the person telling us is the One who made us. And I think that He might have a better idea about it than Instagram, Facebook, the people at work, the kids in our class, or even ourselves.

Within those words we are told that we are:

-Blessed
-Chosen
-Holy
-Blameless
-Loved
-Predestined
-Adopted
-Redeemed
-Lavished upon
-United to God in Christ
-Given an inheritance
-The glory of God
-Sealed by the same Holy Spirit who rose Christ from death

I'm in college to be a teacher as I have said earlier. So here is your homework before you go on to the next chapter, or put the book down and forget to ever finish it. I will never know if you do this or not, but I ask you to. No matter where you find yourself.

I want you to fill in the blank spaces with your name. (If you just find writing in a book to be next to heresy, or if you got this book as a gift and are reading it first, then you can write it out somewhere else.) And then read it out loud. It has to be out loud, that's the homework. It will be awkward the first time. And probably the second time as well. But the assignment it to do it at least once a day for a week.

I promise you that if you do this you'll begin to see yourself differently, or should I say correctly…

Blessed be the God and Father of my Lord Jesus, who has blessed me, ____________________, in Christ with every spiritual blessing in the heavenly places, even as He chose me, ____________________, in Him before the foundation of the world, that I, ____________________, should be holy and blameless before Him. In love He predestined me, ____________________, for adoption as His child through Jesus Christ according to the purpose of His will, to the praise of His glorious grace, with which He has blessed me,____________________, in the Beloved. In Him I, ____________________, have redemption through His blood, the forgiveness or my trespasses, according to the riches of His grace, which He lavished upon me, ____________________, in all wisdom and insight making known to me, ____________________, the mystery of His will, according to His purpose, which He set forth in Christ as a plan for the fullness of time, to unite all things, in Him, things in heaven and things on earth. In Him, I, ____________________, have obtained an inheritance, having been predestined according to the purpose of Him who works all things according to the counsel of His will, so that I,____________________, who have hoped in Christ might be to the praise of His glory. In Him I,____________________, heard the word of truth, the gospel of my salvation and believed in Him and I, ____________________, was sealed with the promised Holy Spirit, who is the guarantee of my inheritance until I fully acquire it, to the praise of His glory.

PRAYER:

Abba,
You have made me for Your glory.
And when I anything else becomes my identity,
I become broken because of it.
I know that the greatest sin I have is not trusting You.
For is Union with Christ is the greatest thing I could obtain,
Then to not trust that I am unified with His is the greatest of all Sin.
I can see that no matter what sins I commit,
There is none so damaging as disunion with Christ through Unbelief.
Lord, keep me from this break and damaging sin.
For in my strength I can never remain here at all times.
I know that when you take those things I find identity in,
You do it because You love me and will not leave me in my Sin.
My sin of know thanking You for everything I have been Given.
My sin of not seeking myself only as a steward of what is Yours.
My sin of trusting myself and forgetting my need of You.
So often I turn Your gifts into my gods,
And those are the ones which hurt me the most.
And their greatest damage is being able to keep them.
Remind me that You are acting for my good and Your glory,
When you take those things I love and worship.
In Your love you take back blessings that I misuse.
Abba, remove the things in my life that cause me sin.
Even those that I love the most.
Let me desire to be more like Jesus more than anything.
Let me desire it even if it hurts in the moment.
The more I see Your love,
The more I desire to love You.

The more I am miserable when I feel removed from it.
Let me hunger and thirst after and understanding of my Union.
Teach me to seek You, and let me find You when I do.
Let me heart be truly broken when I sin,
That I may remember that only death is found in it.
My greatest evil is that I so quickly forget my sin,
And in doing so I forget the ways You have saved me from Them.
Above all else, keep my heart from unbelief.
For without Your help that is my natural state.
Let me always remember my Union with Christ,
Until I am Home and need reminded no longer[10].

---

[10] Adapted from 'Union With Christ' in The Valley Of Vision Prayer Book

IX
Rerouted

"And He made from one man every nation of mankind to live on all faces of the earth, having determined allotted periods and the boundaries of their dwelling place, that they should seek God, and perhaps feel their way towards Him and find Him. Yet He is actually not far from each one of us." –Acts 17:26-27

"The truth is, of course, that what one regards as interruptions are precisely one's life."
–C.S. Lewis

As the summer of 2018 started so did a small little church plant in Alabama[1].

It's the church I am now going to. I'm not the pastor. I haven't led a small group. I don't have any leadership role at all. I've simply shown up each time I have been able, and I think I might have turned into the guy who does sound and the slides during our gatherings. Which means I click the arrow key on pro-presenter and look around frantically if something with the sound goes wrong. I also get to be a big-brother/weird-uncle to some of the kids that come. That part might be my favorite at the moment.

But the fact that we started when we did was not at all lost on me. It almost felt as if was God was playing a joke on me. Not the mean type, the type that my dad used to play on me. The type that lets me know He's there and we can both eventually chuckle about it.

As I have said before, when I first got to Oregon one of the things that I did with the pastors there was set up a timeline for me. One that started with me in that office and one that

---

[1] www.unionchurchao.com

ended with a launching a church plant in Brooklyn, NYC. And the end of that timeline was the summer of 2018. Not only did the timeline end the same season as this church in Alabama was launching, it ended on the very week.

So here I was, sitting in a living room with a group of people I really didn't know and a church plant that wasn't 'mine'. The irony of that wasn't quite lost on me. I wonder if Abba chuckled a little bit when that first timeline was drawn on the West Coast. I think He might have. Again, not at all in a mean way. Although I definitely had times when I saw it that way, even now I sometime struggle not to. More than I would like to share.

When I first got back to Alabama I didn't do much future planning for a few months. I spent that time trying to talk to a girl that I couldn't admit to myself had long decided that we weren't going to talk anymore. But as soon as I started to think of what my life would look like, a life without her, I made plans to get up to the City[2]. I knew some people I could talk to about a possible job and was even talking to one of my friends about a good time to move up. He was even keeping his ear to the ground for a spot that I could have my dog in. Then I even looked up how much I could get for my car knowing I wouldn't need one there. Hoping that what I could get for it might last a month while I got on my feet.

But while I was talking to him I went with my older brother to be his assistant for an art install. We went up to Florence, AL for the Shindig[3]. Looking back he really didn't need an assistant. He was just being a good brother who was, rightfully so, worried about me at the time. He figured that a

---

[2] New York City. There are other places that are great cities, but there is only one place that truly is "The City." At least on this side of glory…

[3] https://www.billyreid.com/the-shindig-archive

weekend away would be a good thing for me. Something to get my mind off of what I had just gone through. That Sunday while we were up there I found a church to go to while everyone else was still hung-over from the lake party. And whenever I travel I always check the Acts 29 website for a church nearby. And there was one, just a few miles away. So I went.

Honestly I can't even remember the name of the church. I can't remember what the sermon was on. I couldn't tell you a single song they sung that morning. I do, however, remember that this was a church that genuinely made me feel welcome though I was someone who had never before darkened their door. And that is something which is an oddity these days. Especially in the South.

I worshiped. Or at least I tried to.

I filled out a prayer card and dropped it in the offering plate. I really didn't think that anything would come of it. I had visited a few churches earlier in the summer, filling out similar cards in each one and never heard a thing in return. So this was going to be just one more attempt for some kind of answer that I already knew wasn't going to come.

But a few days later I was sitting in a local coffee shop back in Auburn with my little sister and got a call from a number that I didn't recognize. I almost didn't answer, assuming that the person on the other line wanted to talk to me about student loans, sweepstake cruses, or chronic illness. To my surprise it was the pastor from that church in Florence.

I can remember a few things from talking to him. The first was that he sounded truly hurt for me. I had filled out the prayer card, saying something to the extent of my wedding fell through and I felt lost. And he took the time to pray for me enough before calling me that when he did he was genuinely hurt because I was hurt. I didn't even know this guy. It was almost as if we were part of the same family or something like that. The other thing I can remember is feeling bad for taking up his time. He was a church planter, and I knew that chances were I would never again be at his church. And I told him so. I told him I lived in the Auburn/Opelika area a few hours south of him and that I would let him get back to matters closer at hand.

When I told him this he told me that he knew a guy who was coming to Auburn/Opelika to plant a church. We got off the phone and then I called that guy.

Looking back, I'm surprised that I didn't scare the guy away. I couldn't have picked him out of a crowd of two people and had only gotten his number a few minuets before. But on the phone that day back in September of 2016, a few days before what I once thought would be my wedding day, I told him I was in. I don't even think he asked me to be; I just volunteered myself.

It's a funny story now. One that he even shared at our launch service for the church plant. But at the time I wasn't even 100% sure why I had done it. But I had been asking over and again was why Jesus brought me back to Alabama. I wasn't the one in the relationship who wanted to live back in Alabama. And yet I was the one that got left here by way of Oregon. I was looking around at all that was happening. Standing in what I 'knew' to be the ruin of the rest of my life and was trying to make sense of it.

My plans had been interrupted and I was just grasping at straws as to why it could have worked out that way.

So I talked with this pastor for a while and then we kept in touch. His plan was to be down in my neck-of-the-woods within the coming months. But six months turned into eighteen. And all the while I was just waiting around. Waiting for some pretty girl to walk into my life or back in, and for Chris to get here so we could plant a church. As I shared in the last chapter these were two things which I had built my identity on, and I was just waiting for my life to start back. And as far as I was concerned that would only happen when Jesus gave me back what He had taken away from me.

But if you've read this far, you know that's not what He had planned. He had something that would be much more painful. He is the great Surgeon, and as much as I objected, as much as I promised I was fine, He knew that there was a surgery that I needed. That there were things which needed to be opened up and things which needed to be taken out.

So while I was waiting around for this church to start was also when my dad talked me into taking classes at the local community college. Looking back I think it was part my parents knowing what was best, as parents sometimes do, and part them just wanting me to be busy and around other people while I was claiming to not be as broken and depressed as I was.

If I wasn't depressed I was certainly suffering from what the old writers called 'melancholy'. Maybe you have been in that place, maybe you are there now. But when I was there the last thing I wanted to do was to be around other people. I was fine with a roommate who wanted to play a game of chess on the porch more days than he didn't. And that was enough for me. In seasons like this we want to isolate. Or at least I did. Maybe you're the one person in this season who doesn't. And if that is you, I'm gonna' have to call bullshit.

But isolation is more than just being alone. Even more depressing is when you're alone in a crowd. And we do whatever it takes to not let people know that's actually going on. I think that's why people so often say at the funerals of people what have committed suicide that they never saw it coming. We have created a culture, especially in the church, where depression is equal to receiving the pirate's black spot. Which we all should have learned from the Muppets can easily result in our tavern being burned down. And that's if we're one of the lucky ones.

So I began to take classes at the local community college. And when I did so I also started going to RUF (Reformed University Fellowship) on Auburn University's campus. And when I went I told myself every reason why I shouldn't be there. I was 26 at the time, and was the second oldest person in the room. Second only to the campus pastor. I was the guy in the back who hadn't been with these people for years. But even in this space I found some people who I am happy to call friends. People like Anne, who was one of the first people to stop me after I told her I was doing well. She called me on it and asked again. Something that I learned from her, and to do from time to time for others. I became friends with Nick, who is now her husband. A feat I'm still not sure how he accomplished.

It was in this fall that I ended up getting back together with my ex for a few weeks. I've spoken of that a little before now, so I won't tell the whole story again. But we got back together. And then history found a way to repeat itself.

And just like that, I was rebroken. But when I look back I can see that I had so many 'what if's' that I would have driven myself crazy. The first time we broke up I wanted to do anything I could to get her back. I prayed and prayed that God would make everything work out the way that I wanted it to work out. The second time around Abba showed me that if He answered those prayers, it wouldn't be a loving thing. Not that she's a terrible person. There is still a part of me that loves the parts of her that made me want to marry her. Maybe there always will be. Maybe that's ok. But we were different people. And looking back we each allowed ourselves to become the person the other wanted to love. And in doing so neither of us was able to truly receive the love that was given, and neither of us was able to see that at the time. At least I wasn't.

After that second break up I didn't know what to do. I was working at a local coffee shop where I closed up each night, and we were open will midnight. So my schedule gave me the same amount of sleep that everyone else has, but I just had the sunrise as my bedtime most days. So I always woke up after noon, and I spent too much time alone. And I drank too much. I would get off of work and just want to not be alone, and after 1am in a college town the only place to go was a bar or pizza spot. So I got in the habit of a beer or two and a slice of pie after most shifts.

It's funny how quickly things can get out of hand when we are not looking for the roots of an action. I was lonely, and that is something that is still a prevailing feeling for me now. But then I just 'needed' to be around people. I needed to know that I was wanted. And so I would go wherever I could to feel as though I was wanted. I was still angry at God, and so any idea that He accepted me just didn't seem to matter.

I don't think that this desire to be wanted is, at the root, a bad thing. God created us in His image. In the image of the only perfect community that has ever existed, the Trinity. That's why shows like How I Met Your Mother and Parks & Rec. are so popular. They aren't the things that tell us that we need community. They are popular because something deep inside of us knows that we need it. Because we were created for it.

I had grown accustomed to someone to talk to each night. I didn't realize how much I would miss simply having someone to tell my day to, and having someone trust me with the actions and emotions of theirs. I'm not even sure I knew that this was what I was feeling at the time.

Through that fall I was going to counseling with Dr. Gary. It's funny; I never really thought that I would become someone who is such an advocate for counseling. But a good biblical counselor can be worth their weight in gold. Just make sure you read the words 'good' and 'biblical'. Because there are a lot out there that have one of those words but not both. Don't go to any of those. They'll leave you just as they found you, only with less money in your bank account.

I could speak about a lot of the stuff that I worked through with Dr. Gary. He was the one that really was able to bring me to the place I spoke of earlier, looking back on that second break up. But a lot of that deals with a story that is not mime to share. So I won't share it here.

A few months later I was able to work at another coffee shop that was closer to my house. Walking distance. It was in that next year that I also began to form some close relationships with people I now consider my family. Guys like Malcolm who I mentioned earlier in the book. I'm even going to get to stand next to him at his wedding in a few months. And even though I haven't stayed at a wedding though the dancing in over two years, I'm exited for this one to be when it happens. And who knows maybe I can show up with someone to dance with. Or maybe not, either way I think it'll be a good time.

I also was able to become friends with Jake. We worked a lot of those closing shifts at the coffee shop together, and since he was in a long distance relationship at the time we spent a lot of late nights having the type of conversations that make me think that if I ever end up having a wedding he'll be there. And, when his now wife moved back in town we kept spending a lot of late night over pizza and beer after closing up. Because I don't care what anyone says, no matter how much you and your fiancé love Jesus, you won't act like him watching a movie after midnight. Something that I know all too well, and something that I often told Jake I knew all too well.

I started spending a lot of my late nights with Rachard. He gets off work around the time that it turns from pm to am. In a lot of ways we are walking the same road. And if there is someone that I would want to pray with, this would be the guy.

This past summer we were talking about birthdays and his was coming up soon. As we spoke he let it be known that he wanted to go camping, for the first time. And I really wasn't sure if I wanted to teach him to pitch a tent. So we ended up staying in this little hunting cabin named 'the love shack[4]'. And I'm still not sure how I feel about that being the sign that hung over a hunting shack in the middle of Little Texas, Alabama. But it had room for the two of us, Nick, and my dog Bella. Nick had to leave early the next morning for marriage counseling with that aforementioned girl who's now his lovely bride. But that night after dinner we prayed.

We prayed like I hadn't prayed in a good long while. It was the type of prayer that made you want to open your eyes because you could tell Jesus was sitting there with you. When it was all said and done we went for almost three hours. I'm not sure I've prayed for that long since. It was the first time that Nick ever prayed to 'Abba'.

We talked about it before hand. When I first started praying that way, directing them to my 'Abba', it felt a bit awkward.

---

[4] The man who owns the cabin has the last name 'Love'. So the name is kinda funny and, I think, meant to be a joke on everyone that he lets stay there.

I had always made joked about people who prayed like that. But the more I did I started to realize something.

If we were to meet, and I hope that maybe one day we can, I would love to tell you about my father. He's one of my heroes. Or I could tell you about my mother. She truly is one of the most amazing women I have ever met. But that's how I would talk about them. I might go into 'dad' or 'mom' once we began to talk. But no matter how much I told you about them, you'd never be able to call my father 'pops'. That's my name for him. You wouldn't be able to call my mother 'momma'. Those are intimate names. Those names mean that I belong to them, and they belong to me. In a way that is unlike any other relationship.

And I have found it's the same in prayer, at least for me. Father is a formal term. Jesus taught us often about His Father in Heaven. But then He did for us what I'll never do for you. He told us that we can use His word, we can call Him 'Abba'. We were welcomed into the place where only the intimate seems appropriate.

For two years I kept taking classes at the community college here in town, and it was only in my last semester that Noah, my pastor at 1st Pres. Opelika, lovingly rebuked me for believing the lie that my life was still on hold. Reminding me that my life was happening before me. That what I had seen as an interruption was in fact, my life. And that life was to be lived.

But being able to live my life meant that I would have to be honest about where I was. It meant that I would have to stop reopening my wounds. Though I am sure I have not taken my last cut from the scalpel of the Great Physician, nor am I naïve enough to think that I have taken the last cut to which I shall only be able to answer "Et tu..?" But I had to allow myself to let these wounds heal. At least I started acting like that's what I wanted; at least most of the time.

A few months ago when I first began to write this I wasn't sure what would become of it. Maybe this was just what I needed to allow those wounds to be scars. I can't remember who I was listening to, but in a sermon I recently heard[5] the pastor was speaking about the difference between scars and wounds. When we are wounded we are vulnerable. We are still in a place where we can't move or act like we once could, or like we will be able to again. We are in a place where we have to weigh each thing we do and where we still feel the pain of what happened each time we move. We react to anything that could touch these places since they are still tender. But scars are different. Scars simply show that though we have been wounded we have lived to tell about it. Some scars show people a path to avoid. Some scars tell people that you have suffered a similar blow, and because of it you are able to show them that they'll live to see their wounds turn to scars as well.

My prayer is that this book will be able to do both. I have tried to show you all of me. At least all of me that pertained to this season which I have been traveling through. I have other stories, but maybe that means I need another project in the future. But these pages began as I was still wounded. And now as I am ending them, I am able to show you my scars. They shall always be there as a reminder of my wounds. And as such they will bring back memories.

---

[5] I believe that it was either from Renovation Church in Atl, The Village Church in TX, or Epiphany Fellowship in Philly. Mostly because those are the podcasts I listen to each week. Well, other than NPR stuff, Myths & Legends, Hardcore History, and Fictional. It also might have been Derek Devine at Apostles Brooklyn, but I don't listen to them every week. Although, if my plan wasn't to move to NYC to start a church my plan would be to move there at sit under Pastor Derek at Apostles.

And that old Counting Crows song still proves true, "The price of a memory is the memory of the sorrow it bring[6]." But even that tends to fade if you will let it. And even two years later, not all my wounds have scared over. But a lot of them have. And that makes me believe that the rest shall follow eventually, even as I limp along.

While staying up to write this evening, well the sun has come out so I guess it is now last night, I noticed that I was drinking from a mug from Black Eye Coffee Shop in Denver, Colorado. I got it while I was still dating my ex. We road-tripped out for a wedding I was in. There was a season where everything I saw that she had given me was walked to the trashcan. But the mug is still sitting next to me. And no matter what came after that memory, that day was a good one. And I'm at the place where I am able to smile at the good memories, no longer allowing them to be tainted by the ones which came after.

I know that is not something that can happen for each person. I know that some of you have a brokenness that is rooted in things which hold no good memories at all. But I believe the ability to see the good is a gift which comes from the Spirit, and with a lot of practice.

Seasons of allowing a wound to scar over can often feel like an interruption. Somewhere that is simply a holding place until we are healed enough to live again. A interim space.

My dad and me often swap books. The last one he gave me I finished earlier today. But as I was thinking about this chapter yesterday I had the book with me. And while

[6] The line is taken from the song Mrs. Potter's Lullaby on the album This Desert Life, which is still one of the best 'start-to-finish' road trip albums there are. If you haven't listened to it start to finish while driving through the night you're missing out.

preparing for the end of my book I found myself in the end of someone else's. Near the end of this story the author, Preston Yancey, wrote these words. And I hope that he'll be ok with me stealing them as I approach the end of this story, "There is a lot of dwelling in this interim space. Dwelling and waiting are different things. To dwell is to believe that you are rooted for a time, perhaps a long time, and you create routine and there is method in this space. To wait is simply to anticipate, there is no need for routine or even method, except to distract. I am being pulled into the place of dwelling; in the rhythm of the church year and the cycles of the daily offices, I am to dwell.[7]"

So I shall invite you, as I was invited. If you are in a space where it seems as though you are simply waiting for life to begin or start-over, learn to make the most of it. Learn that even here you may find life. Learn dwell, even in these places.

So this is where I will leave you. You still have a chapter left. But that is one that I wrote some four months ago. When you pass me by and get there you shall see why. It may not be correct to write the last chapter of a book when you are half-way done writing. But this is my book. And that is how I have done it.

This chapter is unlike the other chapters I have written. And that is intentional. I was told when I first began writing that I needed to write with someone in mind. As I thought of whom I should, or could write to, I could only think of a single person. A person who was wounded; a person who thought that maybe brokenness had become the place that he would forever call home. A person lost not even sure if he wanted to be found, or if it was worth hoping to be found. Because he

---

[7] Yancey, Preston. "Tables." *Tables In The Wilderness*, Zondervan, 2014, p. 220.

knew all too well that the pain of being hopeless can at times be less painful than when hope leaves you feeling broken.

So, I wrote this book for me. It's the one that I wished that someone had placed in my hands two years ago. And if nothing else this chapter will stand as my own Ebenezer the next time I have to walk in the dark. It is a testament that even when we feel interrupted, we are still living, whether we accept that or not. Whether we are able to even be able to. I hope that my story has been able to help you. And I hope that you see this chapter for what it is intended to be, a testament to you that life is happening now even while you are wounded. As your wounds slowly turn to scars. And that there is no shame is being someone with scars to show. For after all, we believe that true life was only available because someone was wounded for us, and He'll proudly wear His scars for all eternity.

PRAYER:

Abba,
You are the Lord of the Oceans and the Seas.
My tiny ship is sailing on a restless sea.
Let Jesus be close to me and guide me safely.
Let no strange or familiar currents drive me off Your course;
Keep me safe on this long and hard journey,
Keep my faith from being wrecked in the storms of life,
Guide me safely to Heaven's harbor.
I ask You for great things,
I expect great things from You,
I know that I shall receive great things.
My only hope is placed upon You.
Hope that You'll be the wind to push me onward.
Hope that You'll be with me when the sun shines on my face.
Hope that You shall be the anchor that keeps me safe.
Hope that You shall be me defense from any violence.
I know that this journey will be long.
The waves of doubt will be high.
The storms of life will often rage around me.
But this is the great thing I ask, knowing You will give.
Let me be held steady, even when all seems lost.
Remind me that Your Word secured my safe passage Home.
Give me Your grace to push me ever onward.
Let me not forget that my arrive Home is already secured.
This day will bring me closer to Home.
Let me be consistent in all of my actions.
Let peace flow through me as the tide.
Let Your righteousness wash over me like the waves.
Help me to live vigilantly,
Give me the skill to turn every care and fear into prayer.
Teach me to be gentle and loving in this path,

Smooth out each stone of my anger.
Let me not forget that You are with me each time I am hurt,
Be the one that I run to, to bind all of my wounds.
Let Jesus ever be near me to quiet the storms.
Let this world be a happier and better place because I lived in
It.
Let my ship always be faced towards the cross.
Let the only waves that reach me,
Be the waves of grace that flow from Jesus' side.
Help me, protect me in this violent sea,
Until I step out on Heaven's shore with never-ending praise[8].

---

[8] Adapted from 'Voyage' in The Valley Of Vision Prayer Book

LUX

X
Light

"In this you rejoice, though now for a little while, if necessary, you have been grieved by various trials, so that the tested genuineness of your faith—more precious than gold that perishes though it is tested by fire—may be found to result in praise and glory and honor at the revelation of Jesus Christ."
-1 Peter 1:6-7

"If you are in Christ, your scars will not have the last word over your life. His scars will."
–Sarah Walton

I am writing this last chapter in much the same way as I wrote the first. I am sitting at the same desk, in the same chair, in the same room, at the same late hour of the night. I am smoking a pipe, possibly the same tobacco[1], although tonight I am drinking a chamomile-mint tea instead of a beer. I am still, in most ways, in the same season of life. I am still single, still pretty broke, still trying to move out of the house I'm in, still wrestling with all of these things. And if I am honest, often times they are still quite hard to deal with. Harder than I would like to admit.

Though I can't point to the exact day that I started writing I will probably remember today for a long time to come. Not because it's the day I'm writing the last chapter of this book, but because it was today, two years ago, that I got a call that changed my life. A call that set everything I was building up in flames.

I am not going to give you the church lie that says that I can look back now and 'count it all as joy' because I can't do that. These last two years hurt like a son-of-a-bitch. They

---

[1] Stockbye's Bulls Eye & Navy Flake have been my favorite smoke for well over a year now and I smoke them far more than anything else.

hurt in ways that I hope that you will never have to feel, but again, if you are reading this, and if you have gotten this far, I assume that you have. Or worse still, you feel that now.

When I was first thinking about writing a book I talked about the idea for some time with my dear friend Bryan. Once while talking about it he told me that I needed to have someone in mind in writing it. That if I tried to write to everyone I would be writing to no one at all. So as I thought about who I wanted to write to, and as I said in the last chapter, only one person kept coming to my mind. And so this entire book has been written with that one person at the forefront of my mind. I wrote this book to myself. I wrote this book to myself because I have not written this book as someone who has completely come through the 'dark night of the soul' but someone who is still, in may ways, going through it. Though it seems as though I can see the dawn beginning to break forth. The sun has not yet risen on the night I have walked through, but it's not as dark as it once was.

I am sure that you have, as I have often done these past two years, had sleep stolen from you. And in those times it seems as if the night gets darker and darker. The streets grow empty and there is a feeling that you are alone. But each time this happens there comes a point where it starts to get a little bit lighter. A little bit less dark. Often for me I don't even begin to notice this until the sun has come up above the horizon.

It doesn't matter what we are doing, or how dark the night before had gotten, the sun always comes up. Every time. Light drives out darkness. And that is the major reason for the name of this book. 'Lux.' For those of you who don't know Latin, and I am among you—I simply know a few small phrases, lux translates to light. More specifically, the title of this book comes from a phrase that became prevalent during the Protestant Reformation, 'Post Tenebras Lux'—'After Darkness Light'. I came across the phrase and wrote it upon my arm[2] to remind myself each day that this was true. For even though I couldn't honestly say that this was something that I had fully experienced, it was still something I knew to be true. Because I know that God is true. And I know that His word is true. Both for me and for you. If you are in Christ, there will be light after this darkness. No matter how long the darkness lasts, or how dark it gets.

But even with that being true, there is still the question, 'Why?' For me this was a question that came back to my mind time and again. I looked back over my life since Christ had brought me to Himself and thought that I had done pretty good. I can in no way say that I was perfect, not by a long shot. But I looked back and though that I had done more than a lot of people, and more than most who were anywhere close to my age. More than a lot of people that seemed to not even care that they had the things that I was broken for not having. I looked at all this and I came, time and again, to that question. 'Why?'

I'll be honest, in this season, as I have already written, I was ready to punch the next person who came up quoting Romans 8:28. I was asking hard questions and I needed hard answers. I am in the theological camp that believes that Christ cannot ever lose one of His own, this is mainly based on Jesus Himself saying just that[3]. But trust me when I say that this question got me as close to that point as I believe I could ever go. Though He promises to never lose me, I tried pretty hard to run away. I cried out in ways that I am ashamed to even remember. But I cried out, because all around me God

---

[2] This is a literal statement; I have the phrase tattooed on my left forearm right above the 5 Solas.

[3] John 6:36, John 10:28, John 18:9

seemed to remain quiet. And though the words on my own arm proclaimed the truth, the voice in my heart did not.

I needed an answer to that question. And I believe that you need that answer as well. But I must be honest, I have no new and profound words. Something that I'm sure you must know well by this point in the book. But what will answer that question of 'why' is not something new. It's not some new conference, or speaker, or writer. We come to find the answer by going back to that which is old. We must come back to the truth of the gospel. We must become gospel fluent[4] in the conversations we have with ourselves. And for me one of the things that brought me back to that point was something that I read.

"'If anyone would come after me, let him deny himself and take up his cross and follow me[5].'For those whom the Lord has chosen and condescended to welcome into fellowship with Him should prepare themselves for a life that is hard, laborious, troubled, and full of many various kinds of evil. For it's the will of their heavenly Father to test them in this way so that He might prove them by trials. Having begun this way with Christ, His only-begotten Son, He continues similarly with all His children. For although Christ the Son, beloved before all other—the one in whom the Father's soul delights—we nevertheless see how little ease and comfort Christ experienced…Why, then, would we exempt ourselves from the same situation to which Christ our head was

---

[4] "To become fluent in a new language, you must immerse yourself in it and commit to practicing it, over and over again. You must use it everyday until you actually start to think about life through it. Becoming fluent in the gospel happens the same way—after believing it, we have to intentionally rehearse it (to ourselves and to others) and immerse ourselves in its truths. Only then will we start to see how everything in our lives, from the mundane to the magnificent, is transformed by the hope of the gospel." –Jeff Vanderstelt

[5] Matthew 16:24b

subjected—particularly since He was subjected to suffering for our sake to provide for us a pattern of patience in Himself? ...'Not only that, but we rejoice in our sufferings, knowing that suffering produces endurance, and endurance produces character, and character produces hope[6],' Believers, being upheld by God's hand, experience this truth while they patiently endure such times. For they're unable to endure such suffering in their own strength. Therefore, as saints endure suffering, they experience God's providing of the strength He has promised to give in times of need. And so their hope is also made strong. It would be ungrateful for them not to expect that they'll discover—in the end—how constant and sure God's truth is. We see now how many related benefits are born from the cross. The cross destroys the false notion of our own strength that we've dared to entertain, and it destroys that hypocrisy in which we have taken refuge and pleasure. It strips us of carnal self-confidence, and thus humbling us, instructs us to cast ourselves on God alone so that we won't be crushed or defeated...It's no little thing to be stripped of our blind self-love and thus to be made aware of our own weakness.[7]"

I am not fool enough to think that these words will be any type of silver bullet that will give a once-for-all answer to your questions or mine. In fact, I know that they didn't do that for you, because they didn't do that for me. But what did happen is that I began to see all of my pain, my suffering, my questions in a different light. Just as when the dawn begins to break, there isn't enough light to see everything clearly. But there is enough light in the pre-dawn sky to begin to walk

---

[6] Romans 5:3-4

[7] Denlinger, Aaron C., and Burk Parsons. "Bearing Our Cross Is A Part Of Self Denial." *A Little Book on the Christian Life*, by John Calvin, Reformation Trust Publishing, A Division of Ligonier Ministries, 2017, pp. 57–63.

around again without bumping into everything. And that's what I was able to start doing, and it is what you will be able to do as well. For it's only when we begin to see our suffering in light of a Savior who suffered will we be able to understand it. I don't know if everything will come to light. And I'm not in the camp that even believes we will have all of our questions answered when we finally see Jesus face-to-face. But this is mostly because I believe that when we get to that point, a lot of our questions just won't seem to matter all that much anymore. So neither will the answers.

But as life goes on and each new day comes, there is a point where we shall all find that it's a bit easier to trust Jesus. There comes a day when we see that we have been praying more, worshiping more, trusting more. But this is not something that comes easy, which means that it's something that lasts[8]. But it's in the fighting for it that things begin to change. I'm not saying that we should fight in an attempt to become perfect, or even better, but that we should fight to see Jesus rightly. And in doing that we'll begin to see ourselves rightly too. Or, as Steve Brown once put it, "Christians really aren't perfect, together, faithful, and wonderful people...but we are loved. That's the truth and the gospel. Are we getting better? Probably, but sometimes the process is so slow that it's hard to notice. But we are loved, forgiven, and accepted. It's His goodness, not ours.[9]"

For me one of the most drastic things that has happened in this season is how much I have begun to pray. I have learned to pray as if my life depended upon it, for it was in this season that I first truly saw how much it did.

---

[8] I have written a bit more on that idea. If you would like you can find that here: https://www.achosensinner.com/single-post/2018/06/06/Fight

[9] Brown, Stephen W. "The Devil Made Me Do It!" *Three Free Sins: Gods Not Mad at You*, Howard Books, 2012, p. 172.

It's easy in hard and painful seasons to ask the questions 'Why?' and 'What If..?' And both of those questions very well have their place. But often when we allow those questions to fill us they become what drive us. We can begin to feed upon them and find our identity in the sadness and brokenness caused by them. It least, as I know all too well, that I can. We allow it to even become our identity, not knowing what to do when those feeling aren't there. But when these questions come to mind they also present us with chances to change the narrative. For if we allow these questions to be left unchecked, they will always drive us to despair. Often we want to believe the lie that God won't give us more than we can handle. Which is something that no part of Scripture actually says[10]. We want to be able to figure it all out on our own, and get it all right again. And then we come to God acting as if we can fool Him into thinking that things are ok again. As if He's someone in the church lobby on Sunday morning.

But when we take a look at what Scripture says, we begin to see another picture. In the first chapter of Isaiah we can see God saying something that is so often left out of our modern Christian-culture. God tells his people to come and reason with Him[11]. In this light, each temptation to go down the roads of why and what-if now become an opportunity to come before the Throne of Grace and reason with God. For the temptation is to trust that things would be better had this thing not happened to us, or if that person had not done whatever, or if I had this thing that I want to have. We can search within ourselves all we want. But no amount of Yoga studios or the Oprah channel telling you to look within will be able to answer the questions you have. For when we walk

---

[10] https://www.desiringgod.org/articles/why-god-gives-us-more-than-we-can-handle

[11] Isaiah 1:18

through the dark night of the soul, all that lies within us is more darkness. To be able to get back to the light, we have to admit that. We don't need to wait around for our eyes to adjust, we need a light to come on. And learning to run to God and not hide in ourselves, is the first step. That was what it was for me. That is what is was for each person I have talked to, or read, who has gone though a similar situation. And that is what it shall be for you as well.

As much as I would love to say that in pressing into prayer and diving into Scripture you'll be able to find answers to all the questions that you have, but you won't. As much as it feels like knowing the right answer, or even the right question to ask, would be the thing that would be able to draw you out of your own dark night, it won't. It won't because as much as I do believe that God does answers our prayers, I do not believe that is the chief end of prayer. I have begun to learn that the main point in prayer is that we get to come before God. We get to come before Him in ways that even the angels don't have the right to come before Him. We get to come before Him as His sons and His daughters. And in coming before Him, we begin to see Him for who He really it. We begin to find our joy right there, in His presence. We begin to love Him for Him, and not for the things that He has, or may give us. We begin to become more like Him. For that is one of the keys to getting past whatever it is that has brought you to the point of picking up this book. For in prayer, more than answers, we get Him who knows the answer.

Although I know that doesn't always feel like a good deal. There are still times when I find myself asking how long I have to keep coming back to God about the same thing. It's easy to lose focus on this reality. For me it's almost a daily occurrence. But that is one of the many reasons why we also need gospel community. It's not enough to learn to speak truth to ourselves, although that is vital in this life, we must also have those around us who often speak truth. One without the other is like a sword with only one sharp side. When it comes time to use it, you'll just have to pray that the sharp side hits.

At the start of this chapter I quoted Brother Lawrence[12] from his book *The Practice of the Presence of God.* This particular quote was taken from his Thirteenth letter. And more than a quote I would like to allow you to read it in full:

"Dear Friend,

I cannot thank God enough for the way He has begun to deliver you from your trial.

God knows very well what we need and that all He does is for our good. If we knew how much He loves us, we would always be ready to face life—both its pleasures and its troubles.

The difficulties of life do not have to be unbearable. It is the way we look at them—through faith or unbelief—that makes them seem so. We must be convinced that our Father is full of love for us and that he only permits trials to come our way for our own good.

Let us occupy ourselves entirely in knowing God. The more we know Him, the more we will desire to know Him. As love increases with knowledge, the more we know God, the more we will truly love Him. We will learn to love Him equally in times of distress or in times of great joy.

Although we seek and love God because of the blessings He has given us or for those He may give us in the future, let's not stop there. These blessings, as great as they are, will never carry us as near to Him as a simple act of faith does in time of need or trouble.

Let us look to God with these eyes of faith. He is within us; we don't need to seek Him elsewhere. We have only

---

[12] Thanks again for the book, Anne. It truly has been an aid to my wearied soul.

ourselves to blame if we turn from God, occupying ourselves instead with the trifles of life. In his patience, the Lord endures our weakness. Even so, just think of the price we pay by being separated from His presence!

Once and for all, let us begin to be His entirely. May we banish from our hearts and souls all that does not reflect. Let's ask Him for the grace to do this, so that He alone might rule in our hearts.

I must confide in you, my dear friend, that I hope, in His grace, that I will see Him in a few days.

Let's pray for one another.[13]"

If you read the footnote of that chapter it tells you that Abba did answer that last prayer. And only a few days after writing this he no longer had to spend a life trying to practice the presence of God, for he had entered into it fully.

In reading that I hope that you were able to see that same thing that I did when I first read it. We are not promised a life free of pain or suffering or depression or anxiety or fear or anything else. Which should be clear by this point. But it is within the middle of these things that we are called to press into Christ. And it is in these seasons that, when we allow ourselves to, we can feel the presence of God stronger than any other. This does not make the season easy. At times this nearness only makes it where we can wake up in the morning. But in doing so we are able to, if we allow ourselves to see it, declare that Scripture is true when it says that His mercies are new each morning. For I can only assume that you have, as I have, gotten in bed more nights than one with the only prayer being "I'm done". And yet each night that I went to bed, with nothing left, I was able to wake up the next morning. I can't think of a single time I

---

[13] "Thirteenth Letter." *PRACTICE OF THE PRESENCE OF GOD*, by BROTHER LAWRENCE, Whitaker House, 1982, pp. 55–56

woke up shouting the next day praises. But often we so desire a war to be won that we forget to celebrate when a battle is.

Sometimes these battles won can only be seen in hindsight. I can look back over the past few years and see that I have learned a lot. I can look back and see ways that I am more like Jesus, though not nearly as much as I wish I was. I can, by looking back, see a lot has happened in my head, my heart, and in my soul. But I couldn't have pointed to any of that in the moments it was happening. I was simply trying to hold onto Jesus for dear life, and as a result He was close. Or maybe it would be more honest to say He was holding onto me for my dear life. And because He was close, I found myself slowly becoming more like Him than I was before.

And that, more than anything else I've found, is one of the ways out this dark night. So often we desire to ok again. Even getting to the place of desperation where we no longer even desire to be doing good, we simply desire to be ok. Thinking that is the best we could hope for. And in these times it is easy to forget that each day is full of battles. If we have the courage to be truthful, we still lose many of them. More than we would like. At least I do. But I have come to find that I lose the battles which I choose to fight on my own. The one when I don't simply run to Jesus and ask that He fight for me as He has said He would do.[14]

But, if we allow ourselves to see it, our days are just as full of wins. Each day is full of God's grace rolling over us. And when we begin to focus on those things, we begin to see that God is still at work in us, through us, and for us. And it is when we allow ourselves to not only see this, but focus on it that things begin to change. It is here that we begin to refocus our gaze not on where we are, but on who's we are. And, for

---

[14] Exodus 14:14

those of you that belong to Christ, we are holy, blameless, loved, chosen, pursued, and blessed[15].

When we are able to begin to see these things, and begin to see ourselves this way, we are able to find the strength to fight for joy once again. And when we are honest, even this is a gift of grace. Which is a sign that God is still for us no matter how hard that is to believe. And that is a win. Which is another reason to fight. Repeat.

For just as we often get into habits that reinforce, even if we don't notice it at first, our season of darkness. We can fight for, and train ourselves in, habits that will begin to lead us out of it. Though it is only God who can make the sun come up and the night flee, we can work for that end which we know is ours. And to do this we need only trust what Scripture says about us. We need only live like what we already are. One of Abba's own beloved children, whom He loves greatly.

We must get to the place where we see Jesus, the real Jesus of the Bible, as our advocate. As the one who has ordered our steps, the ones which bring joy and the ones which bring pain. For in the end each of them will bring us closer to Him. And when we see Jesus this way, knowing that He truly is the ultimate goal, we will begin to see that even the most painful cuts come from the Great Surgeon taking away that which would kill us, instead of viewing them as the stabs of some enemy in the dark meant to take from us that which gives life.

---

[15] Ephesians 1:3-14 (This might just be my favorite portion in all of Scripture, if you haven't figured that out by now [I even took it out and used other portions of Scripture twice thus far in this book so that I wouldn't sound repetitive. Maybe I need to write my next book on that portion of Scripture.])

That's the way I saw my pain. As a wound from people who said they loved me and seemed not to know what that word meant. And for longer than I wish was true, I counted God among them. But if we trust what the Scripture says, even their ability to raise the knife to our backs was allowed by God. Allowed for our good and for His glory. When we remember this we can begin to ask ourselves the right questions. Instead of 'Why?' and 'What if..?' we are now able to ask 'What are You doing in me?' and 'What are you taking that would have killed me?' Though again, this is not something that is close to easy or anywhere near pain free. But it will lead to life.

God knows us. God loves us. God is for us. This above all must be remembered.

Even though sometimes He puts us through pain that feels like hell, He does so to keep us from actually having to go there. For those of us who belong to Christ, our suffering may feel like hell, but it's the closest to Hell that we'll ever have to go. And as much as it sucks to feel like you're going through hell, it's a great joy to know that we never actually have to. And this is a beautiful grace.

Rosaria Butterfield wrote on the subject of grace in the midst of pain and suffering, "Grace does not make the hard thing go away; grace illumines the hard things with eternal meaning and purpose. Grace gives you company in your affliction in Christ himself and in the family of God.[16]"

So at the end of it all I have to admit that I'm still on this journey with you. I'm still working through some of this

---

[16] "Walking the Emmaus Road." *The Gospel Comes with a House Key: Practicing Radically Ordinary Hospitality in Our Post-Christian World*, by Rosaria Champagne Butterfield, Crossway, 2018, p. 201.

myself. No 'silver bullets' or 'magic oils'. No matter how much I wish there were.

But maybe that's it. Maybe we all need to remember that life is messy. Maybe we all need to admit that we are all a little bit broken. And maybe that's ok. Or, to steal words not my own to describe what I have tried to do in these pages, "I decided to tell my secrets and then to talk about how the cross began to cover, heal, and free me. I talked about forgiveness, sin, and love in a highly improper way. Looking back, I suspect that some of the things I said were rather shocking. And I fully expect to be stoned.[17]" And that is what I have done.

Though this season has been hard, it's not my last season. And it's not your last season either. Whatever hardships you are facing as you read this know that this may be the end of this book, but it's not the end of my story.

And this is not the end of your story either.

[17] Brown, Stephen W. "How's It Working for You So Far?" *Three Free Sins: Gods Not Mad at You*, Howard Books, 2012, p. 22.

PRAYER:

Abba,
You guided Your people through the wilderness by a cloud and By fire.
I feel as though I am a stranger here, with a stranger's lack of Care.
I am nothing more than a pilgrim in this life.
My journey is leading me home to Zion.
My focus is set upon You and the coming again of Your Son, My King, Jesus.
And my heart is Yours, to do with whatever You please…
For you have created it.
You redeemed it.
You renewed it.
You have captured it.
And You have conquered it.
Keep my safe from every enemy of my soul and salvation,
Crush every bit of lust that rises up in rebellion against you,
Kill every sinful passion that often rises up from within me,
Wipeout any desire in me that is from anyplace but You.
Every part of who I am truly comes alive in Your presence,
I love you with my soul, mind, body, strength, might, spirit,
Affection, desire, intellect, and understanding. Forgive me when This is not true of me.
You are the perfection of all perfections.
And from You come all truth and truthful insight.
The little in me which is good comes from Your overflow of Goodness.
Oh Lord, compared to You the sun is but darkness,
Compared to You all beauty is deformed and wretched,
Compared to You the greatest wisdom is ignorance,
And the best that we could ever offer up is filthy and broken.

You deserve love and worship greater than I could ever be able To offer You.
Set my heart on fire with love for You. That I could love You Truly.
Let all of my love and affection be tied to You.
Let the greatest desire of my heart be You.
For only then can I truly walk in honest, endless worship.[18]

---

[18] Adapted from 'Journeying On' in The Valley of Vision Prayer Book

Final Thoughts.

I am sitting down to write this a few months after I finished writing the last words of this book. And about a month since I have finished the editing that I did for it (I know that this book needs more, but I had to do it all myself and sometimes it's hard to catch everything in your own work). The Kickstatrer campaign for this book still has a few days to go, but it just reached it's goal. So no matter how many times I have second thoughts about allowing all of these words to venture out into the world and, Lord willing, take a life of their own any attempts to stop are now null and void.

But there is something quite freeing in that though as well. If you have read this book, then you know that I have, and still do, doubt that God is good or working for my good. I still have to wrestle with the fact the 'big' prayers I am praying for myself are all borrowed from last years prayer list. And to be honest, last year I borrowed them from the year before. I still struggle with feeling like I am the odd man out, even as a part of a church that I know loves and accepts me. And I hope that in knowing all of this you will be given the permission to be as honest as I have been. And maybe even more.

In the past few years the #MeToo movement has been given a tremendous amount of traction. And I think that is a good thing. I think that things are being brought into light that should have been taken there long ago. As I watched this movement begin to grow[1] I couldn't help but wonder why it

---

[1] Like every movement in the history of the world it is full of sinners in need of grace, so if you write off this whole movement because of one or two sinners then shame on you. This is the same line of reasoning that people use to bash the Church. We of all people should know that even the best things on earth are broken things. The Church should be the champion of this movement, praying for it often.

was happening now. And though there are a plethora of reasons why, I think that one is that for so long these women felt alone. And then all of a sudden someone simply said “Me too”. And this is my prayer for this book. It is my prayer that in sharing my brokenness, my sin, and God’s grace that covered them both that many of you will have echoed, me too.

I hope and pray that this book has served as something which has given you the ability to share what you have gone through, the good, the bad, and the grace. I have prayed long and hard that this is not simply my story, but that this book shall become part of your story. I can still remember the first few times I truly encountered pure grace, 1,000 proof strong, and drank fully. It was something foreign to me. And for a time it even felt as though this was some wrong forbidden thing. But new things usually feel this way.

I hope that this book was a taste of that type of grace for you. And I hope that it was a grace that led you to love Jesus more than you had ever done before. Because I can promise you, if He can still loves me…He can still love you.

I also wanted to end this with giving you some of the tools that I was able to place in my tool belt that helped me through this season. Many I have talked about in the book, but as I am able to look back over the past few years I can see that certain things I used and needed for a moment, and others I have used and used again, and plan to use till I am Home and need no more need of any earthy tools.

The first one is an app for my phone called FighterVerse. It’s a scripture memory tool that costs three or four bucks, and it’s worth every penny. As I write this I have less than a hundred dollars to my name and I would buy it again today if I had to. I have tried to memorize scripture a number of different ways but this one, at least for me, stands head and shoulders above everything else I've tried.

Another tool which I have used a lot is more of a habit. And that habit is times of personal worship. I know that it'll be hella awkward. But make a playlist that's at least 20 to 30 minuets long and then proceed to sing those songs to Jesus. The more that you do this the more that you'll believe the truth that worship really is spiritual warfare. And the thrice-holy, triune God of Heaven calls you to do this, and Satan doesn't want you to. Just something to think about. Not trying to guilt or 'judge' anyone. Just throwing out some facts, and you can't argue with facts. Although people often try these days.

The next tool that I have used is prayer cards. I have a wallet that is kinda large made by my friends at Loyal Sticklin. It was made to be able to hold a Field Notes notebook in it, and because of this it's also the right size for index cards. I have a set of these index cards that I have written prayer requests on, and I simply take 2-4 with me each day. I'll take them out when I remember, or see them. And these are not just prayer requests for other people, they are for myself as well.

Another great tool that has helped me is cultivating the discipline of journaling and prayer journaling. I have worked to get to the place that I at least open each of these every day and put something. Some days it has been little more than a sentence, and some days I miss it all together. It also helps to keep these separate, but that is a personal preference. Doing this has forced me to slow down and process what all has happened that day, and then take another journal and orient all of that processing into prayer about what has happened.

The next one I wish didn't even need to be said, but I think it does. And that one is being an active part of a local church. Just showing up on Sunday does little for us. We are called into, and need, a community of people around us who can speak gospel truth to our soul. We also need places where we are able to speak gospel truth. No matter how unworthy you feel doing so, speaking the truth of the gospel to other is something that Abba will use in great ways to heal you.

I could list dozens of other tools that have been helpful, but I will tell you of one more and let you close this book for the last time.

The last tool which has served me in a major way is that of fighting to honor the Sabbath. I don't want to go too deep into a Sabbath debate here, but God clearly states that this should be a day unlike the others in our week. It should be holy. Instead of going into what all should be allowed and what shouldn't I am simply going to let you know how I try (and often fail) to honor the Sabbath and make it different. On Sundays I try to avoid all social media. Though I do nor always do this, I try to avoid it all together. I also only listen to Christian music on this day. I don't think that Christians can't listen to music that isn't Christian, and a quick look at my record collection would prove this, but on Sunday's I set aside any music that isn't leading me into worship of Jesus. I also try to avoid media intake. I love a good Netflix show and I listen to NPR (and their podcasts) for hours and hours each week. Just not on Sundays. I also want to put here that on Sundays I gather with my local church (even though I don't always want to). This should be a given, but these days nothing is. I want to have Sunday feel like it's not just another day of the week. And as such it has begun to truly feel different as I have treated it that way.

I would invite you to try out any and all of these tools. Maybe some will work for you. Maybe they won't. But as I have had people share their tools with me I wanted to return the favor.

Now to Him who is able to keep you from stumbling and to present you blameless before the presence of His glory with great joy, to the only God, our Savior, through Jesus Christ our Lord, be glory, majesty, dominion, and authority before all time, and now, and forever. Amen[2]

[2] Jude 23-24

Acknowledgments

Damn. There are so many people I would like to, and need to, thank in regards to this book. And through the season of my life that this book encompasses. I am going to write the longest acknowledgment section ever and still I am going to forget people.

First, I would like to thank my Momma. Thank you for crying with me and for me. Thank you for letting me smoke my pipe in the house while I was simply needing a safe place to be. You went out of your way to make sure that I was safe, and had a place that was the same. Each time I was at my darkest you were a beacon of light guiding me back home to safe harbor.

Thank you pops. You are the man that I hope to be. And even when we disagree, I would still follow you to the gates of hell with a water gun. You have lived a life that risked it all, me included, for the sake of the gospel. And I hope that if I ever have kids they'll be able to look at me and say that I was half the man that their papaw was. As far as I am concerned, you stand among Luther, Calvin, Dr. King, Spurgeon, Manning, and Athanasius. Anyone who would say different doesn't know you.

Thank you to each of my siblings:
Dreamer, or Rikki as you now like to be called, you allowed me to bellow out my fears to you often. You took on far too much of my pain. I am sorry for that. But you took it and you helped me walk when all I would do was limp. I wanted to always be strong for you. But you reminded me that both of us have Jesus as an older brother who is strong enough for us both.
RC, you have always loved me. Since I was born you looked out for me. You never let anyone harm me. Even when I got drunk and wanted to harm myself; you fought me for two hours and took a gun out of my hands because you love me. And we have that picture of us both with black eyes to show it.
Bingo, I love you kid. You might have the best beard in the family now, but I still can remember you as Legolas running around the Hobbit Wall. You are my little brother, but you are bigger than me

now. We disagree, more than most. But I know that you love me with all you have. And I love you the same. Thank you for never giving up on me. For fighting for me, and with me. Thank you for letting me stand in your corner when you fought. Thank you for being that strong in the cage. And thank you for being that strong in the Blue House when I needed it most.

Bryan Joy, thank you for being my brother. Thank you for being the one to push me to start this. I am a better man because you are in my life. I love Jesus more because you are in my life. You being a part of my life is something I truly consider a gift of grace. I hope that I have kids one day, because I cannot wait to have you be a part of their life. Uncle Bryan from Oregon.

Neal McKinney, thank you for being there for me. Even when you were going through your own shit. You made time to be there for me. I have asked a lot of pastors to disciple me in my life, and you are the only one who never stopped going out of your way to do that. I cannot begin to say how much that means to me. You have been one of the guys I feel the need to call when I am wrestling with anything. When I think of people I want to be like, your name is near the top of that list. Also, thanks for giving enough on Kickstarter to be thanked. So I guess you get twice as many.

Malcolm, Rachard, Jake. You guys are my brothers. I don't know another way to put it. You guys have been my compass on more than one occasion. You have told me your sin and allowed me to speak the gospel over you. And I have told you my sin more often, and each time that happened both of you gave me truth and grace. You never made light of my sin, but you always reminded me that the cross was heavier. Ya'll are so dear to me.

Dr. Gary, thank you for putting up with me time and again in your office. Each time I walked in I wanted to be 'ok' and tried to act that way. And time and again you called me on my shit and called me into life. You were not ok with me wearing a mask, even when I was. Thank you for loving me in that way. It just might have saved my life.

Pastor Noah, thank you for being my pastor. Thank you for being the first person to give me another shot at 'ministry' after my season of being broken. Thank you for all the time we talked over coffee and whiskey. Thanks for believing in me even when I didn't believe in myself. And thank you for calling me on my shit more than once, and more than that…thank you for getting close enough to see my shit. Because we both know I can wear a good mask when I want to. If only you could have got me dunking babies I would've been the best damn Presbyterian you'd ever seen.

Pastor Robert, thank you for sitting in your office for seven hours with me back in Opelika. You were full of grace and truth. Which is another way of saying that you were full of Jesus.

Pastor Chris, thank you for coming to Auburn/Opelika. Thank you for allowing someone you had never met share your vision. You let me be a part of your dream, and for that I thank you.

Glenn, thank you for all the games of chess and the late nights on the Blue House porch. Thank you for sharing my pain and my dreams. You are my family now. I know that you have moved away. But I hold you close. And I also won the last game of chess, so you have to come down soon and avenge that loss...

1st Pres Opelika, thank you for allowing me to call you home. For everyone there who put up with me yelling at Noah and acting more charismatic than you were used to, thank you. You were a place where I found life and healing. I can never pay back what I was given while I was counted as one of you. I simply hope that you know that being seen as a part of your family for the two years I was there is something I take great pride in. And not the kind of pride that turns you bad, but the kind of pride like my momma had. (As much as everyone there loves the Avett Brothers ya'll should get the reference.)

Thank you to everyone that supported my Kickstarter project that allowed me to get this book off my computer and into your hands. It really means so much that anyone would want to read my words.

And I would like to specifically thank Mallory Stein, Andrew Whited, Uncle Ben Morris, Michael Hamilton, Olwyn Buckley (my Irish mum), The Marsh Collective, Mary Rebekah Ardoin, & Ron and Emma Whited.

To you I don't know yet. I pray for you often. And more than that, I pray that Abba makes me the man that I need to be before we meet. I can't wait till you are more than a prayer I feel awkward praying. I can't wait till I can cook you dinner and buy you flowers. This book is the story of a lot, but it is also the story of me trying to become the man that I want to be when we meet.

And lastly, Sarah, I doubt you shall ever read this. But I want you to know that I forgive you. I want nothing but the best for you, and I hope that I will be able to see you one day when I get Home. I hope that you know that. I know that we each sinned with each other and against each other. And I hope you can forgive me for my sins. I understand now that it had to end, I just wish it could have ended differently.

Made in the USA
Coppell, TX
11 February 2021